tell
me no.
I dare
you!

D1637051

tell me no. I dare you!

Scott H. Silverman

CNN HERO AWARD RECIPIENT

BOOKS

TELL ME NO. I DARE YOU!
By: Scott H. Silverman

Copyright © 2010 Scott Silverman

Published by GKS Books, an imprint of GKS Creative
Murfreesboro, TN, 37128
United States of America
gkscreative.com

ISBN-13: 978-0-615-32532-3

MEMOIR / INSPIRATION / SELF-HELP

Library of Congress Control Number: 2008906394

Printed in the United States of America

Acknowledgements

For a portion of my life, I believed I had to do it all myself, that the guiding principle of my life was *no*. In 1984, my life was turned upside down, and I discovered, almost the hardest way, that interdependence, not independence and not dependence, is what gets not just me, but the entire world, to the reality of *Yes*.

Without the following people, I would not be who I am or where I am today.

Mom and Dad, thank you for always being there for me and believing in me, no matter what.

Michelle, my best friend, the mother of my children, and the woman who stood by me in my darkest days and continues to stand next to me as we move into the future, I love you. You have always, always encouraged me to follow my heart and never given up on me. I can never thank you enough.

Jessica Ann and Gracie Sarah, the joys of my life, you are the two reasons I never stopped trying. Thank you. I love you.

Marsi and Stacy, my dear sisters, you have always loved me unconditionally. Greg, my brother, you have always been yourself, and you are always in my heart. To my extended family, thank you for always being there and supporting me throughout the years

My buddies, Jeff L and Tom K, always read and reviewed what I wrote, good or bad. Skip W encouraged me to embark on this journey. Thanks to all of you.

My colleagues, thank you for always trusting the process. I honor you.

And all you whom I have served, you have helped make me who I am, and I thank you for that.

Thank you all very much!

Love, Scott

Contents

Foreword

Anyone who has made an honest commitment to public service understands the power of partnerships. There should be no doubt that the public good is better served by coalitions and links among like-minded individuals and groups. We enhance the power of our communities by building and supporting these partnerships and should applaud all those working to enhance them.

In San Diego, Scott Silverman deserves the applause. He has taken his personal challenges and converted them to strengths. In turn, he has used those strengths to create powerful and resilient partnerships that continue to serve our community very well.

As founder of Second Chance, one of our City's most respected and accomplished social service agencies, Scott has discovered how to bring people together to support others. With extraordinary determination—and a charming disregard for politics—Scott has built a broad network of partners that make Second Chance stronger and better prepared to meet the needs of its clients.

Tell Me No. I Dare You! is Scott's tale of building Second Chance after rebuilding himself. It's a personal story of drug addiction, recovery and the power that comes from choosing *Yes* over no time and time again. Scott's book offers us glimpses into his own life and the lives of those he's served at Second Chance. It shows us the power each of us has to transform the "no" of the moment into the "yes" for a lifetime.

It has been more than a pleasure to work with Scott. It has been an education about the world of the possible. He has added me to his ever-growing network of partners and has taken the time to introduce me to the personal success stories that seem to expand every day at Second Chance. It is all inspiring.

Tell Me No. I Dare You! is an inspirational work too. It has the candor needed to confirm its honesty and is complete with unparalleled insight into the mechanisms of helping ourselves or anyone needing a second chance in life.

Mayor Jerry Sanders
Mayor of San Diego, California

CHAPTER 1

A Yes-Driven Life

No is a word we hear often in life. The toddler hears "no, don't do that." The child hears the same. The adolescent becomes prey to "No, you can't do that," which often segues into the destructive "No, you *can't* do that," the first indications that something is out of reach, of an incapacity to achieve. And it is in that sense that *no* is the enemy of goals, of dreams, of achievement. It is that *no* which often derails us. It is that *no* which I find unacceptable for myself and for society at large. It is that *no* which diffuses our *Yes.*

My motto is: *Go ahead. Tell me no. I dare you!*

Go ahead. I will find a way to get to *Yes.* I vow to do that today; I did it yesterday; I will do it tomorrow. I will find *Yes.* Every day, every week, every year, I hear *no* all around me—"No, it can't be done…No, you don't have enough education…No, there is not enough money…No, it will never work…No. I can't…No, I don't know how." The world is filled with millions of big fat *NOs.*

No is toxic. It is the root of negativity, petulance, and rage. It is drug and alcohol dependence. It is deceit. It is a compromised lifestyle. It is rebellion without a cause. It is accepting less than you deserve. It is, at its core, self-hatred. And yet, it is so comfortable and familiar!

No is neither a concept I accept nor a code I live by. My code is *Yes!* Yes to God. Yes to family. Yes to integrity. Yes to success—my success and yours. I dare myself to say "Yes," and I lead others to say "Yes." I live it always, everywhere. *Tell me no. I dare you!* I have learned to take on the dare. *No* was a force that I almost allowed to destroy me, but I have learned that *no* can also be a tool that drives me to *Yes*, and if I could learn it, so can you.

The Power of *YES*

It is 7:30 on a beautiful California morning in the year 2008. I am driving towards the "other side" of San Diego on my way to the latest graduation at the agency I created to teach people how to step out of *no* and into *Yes*. My anticipation, hope, and excitement mingle, and I smile as I drive even faster. I may have grown a lot in the last twenty years, but I still like *fast*. After fifteen years of helping to give people a Second Chance, I still feel as if I am the one graduating for the very first time. My heart fills with a passion that compels me to jump in and shake people up until they can see the *Yesses* of their own lives.

Those who graduate from Second Chance have learned to turn their *no* into *Yes*—despite powerful odds against them. What would it be like to be nine years old and selling drugs? When Miguel Ruiz was a schoolboy in fourth grade, drugs were his livelihood, and he lived with his mother, a prostitute. There was no father at home—or anywhere as far as Miguel knew—and he made his own rules. By age thirteen, he found a home within a local gang which had its own structure, rules, and recognition. Miguel is a natural-born leader, so he quickly became the gang's top dog. Amazingly, he still earned straight *A*'s in school and even entered college. Believing that rules were made to be broken, Miguel continued the life of a hustler and soon dropped out. When hustling and drugging caught up with him, he was sent to the Arizona Boys Ranch. There, just before he was discharged at age twenty, he heard Jodi Summerson give a presentation on my program, Second Chance. He glimpsed something I call a *speck of light*. I can't really capture this inner fire with words, but it is a light that I believe is the spark of *Yes* we are all born with. By the time Miguel was ready for release from prison, Jodi's message had prepared him to release a life of darkness.

Miguel entered Second Chance in 2003. After graduating from our three-week program, he lived in one of our drug-free safe houses and began to work for a paycheck. His self-respect was born and, with it, a desire to find the man who had fathered him. Miguel and his father were reunited that same year. Miguel has continued his commitment to lead a *Yes*-driven life and teach others. He is currently our number-one trainer at Second Chance where he assists others in finding the commitments that will be in alignment with their *Yes*. His *Yes* eventually translated into direct help for the thousands he has trained.

Jodi Summerson's commitment to *Yes* found its way to Miguel and allowed his hope to be born. She had achieved it herself against remarkable odds, though her story is drastically different. I met her in 2003, when she saw Second Chance as a place to do what she does best: change people's lives. Jodi joined our organization and quickly started planting seeds of hope and forgiveness everywhere she went. She has never been homeless, never been in prison (except to recruit clients for Second Chance), and never had a substance abuse problem. Why did she want to join Second Chance when she had the education and experience to have a career with a more secure financial base?

The fire that burns in Jodi began decades ago in Venice, California where she lived in what psychologists had just begun to call a dysfunctional home. The oldest of seven children, she grew up in an environment colored by drinking, violence, and family jail terms. Yet she danced and dreamed of a life outside the world she knew. Jodi says that reading books put dreams in her head at a very young age, and she knew she wanted more than Venice Beach and a life of chaos. Somehow, Jodi says, she just knew that education was the ticket out, so she focused on getting good grades and excelling in dance.

When Jodi was sixteen, she had a baby, and then she had another at seventeen. Many people would use this kind of heavy responsibility as an excuse to give up and let go of their dreams. Her dream of dancing professionally did end, but Jodi found another dream. She told me that she had not heard the word *benchmark*, yet this seventeen-year-old woman began to set a series of goals for herself: finish high school, get out of her mother's house, and nurture and protect her babies. She was determined that they would have a different life than she had, and she made it happen.

She'd married to get away from her mother, and by the age of nineteen, she had three babies, a husband, and a profitable business typing her friends' and their friends' term papers. The next goal was to get a job and then go to college. During this time Venice, California, was turning into an arena for drugs, drug use, drug wars, and drug deals. Her brothers and brother-in-law and eventually her husband all became involved in buying, selling, and using cocaine and then crack.

Jodi would work all day, come home, and while the front of her house was filled with the chaos of drugs, Jodi would be in a back room reading fairy tales to her children, working puzzles with them, having tea parties with her little girl, and instructing her sons in the ways a man of God acts and behaves. Her husband might be gone for two to four days at a time, sometimes more, but Jodi held their home together for her kids.

All of Jodi's siblings have been to prison. Her three brothers are currently incarcerated, and her sister is caught in an endless treadmill of prison and release. Jodi credits her grandfather's teachings—he was a Baptist minister—with igniting her passionate *Yes* and her three children with keeping her sane and sober. Ask her why she did not go the way of her siblings, and she answers, "Who had time to drink and drug, when you had to be up for work, school, and three beautiful babies who deserved a good life?"

Jodi achieved much of her dream: her daughter is now a supervisor in Los Angeles and her son is a minister. Her second son enrolled in UCLA, and a nearby hospital hired him as an orderly. No drugs, no drinking—but it wasn't enough to protect him. Without warning, he was murdered, shot in the head by two young Hispanics hoping to pass gang induction by getting a kill. UCLA flew its flag at half-mast for Jodi's son, one of the thousands of young people whose bright futures are wiped out in the time it takes a bullet to go from point A to point B.

Jodi had a great excuse to say, "F— it! I give up." Once again, she found another way to express her *Yes*. Always a community activist, she joined Los Angeles Urban League, United Farm Workers, Black Panthers, and a variety of church groups. Jodi decided to focus her career on helping people get productive jobs, believing that if individuals had worthwhile, well-paid jobs, they would be more likely to stay out of gangs and contribute to the world.

What impresses those who meet Jodi is the obvious *Yes* in her heart that translates into an active commitment to never give in and never give up. Driven by passion and compassion, she is like a shark homing in on her target: she will find a hopeless individual and pounce, offering clear goals, a way out of drugs, prison, or street crimes. Demanding a response, she draws people out of the cave of darkness into the light of hope. Nothing gets in this woman's way. She is committed to prisoner re-entry—assisting ex-felons to become part of a productive community—and, to quote her, "I get people out of the self-pity woe-is-me attitude. Get [them] out of [their own] philosophical 'think tanks,' and get into *doing*." She expresses her *Yes* through her ability to change lives, strengthen the community, and open the doors that empower individuals to live productive lives. Her dedication and action help to assure that others will not kill or be killed as her son was.

The world works in funny ways. In Miguel Ruiz, Jodi recruited exactly the sort of individual for whom others in her tragic circumstances might have held an intense hatred, a Hispanic gang-banger. Instead of succumbing to a need for revenge, Jodi focused her powerful *Yes* on keeping a young man from returning to his former gang, not unlike the gang that was responsible for the death of her son. *Yes* won. The young Hispanic man took the hand that was offered—a hand extended out of a powerful commitment to hope. That is what happens with heart-held commitments: they are passed on from person to person to person. Fear-based and hate-based commitments are also passed from one person to another—as we'll discuss in chapter thirteen.

The Power of *YES* in Action

Jodi and Miguel, a wise African-American woman and a young Hispanic, came together because a recovering drug-addicted Jewish man—I, Scott Silverman—followed his *Yes*. My commitment will always be to pass on my programs from a place of *Yes* and from a place in my heart where my highest self resides. We do that every day at Second Chance.

When you visit, you will have a firsthand opportunity to meet some of the devoted individuals who work here and see them do their jobs with genuine interest and love. Any visitor who really watches will see that our people care about who they are and how they do their jobs.

More than anything else, there is one element seen by all visitors that exemplifies what Second Chance is all about. It is The Wall. It stretches thirty-nine-and-a-half feet, end to end. As you arrive at our main entrance and come through the doorway, it is to the left of our central hallway. It is especially important that anyone who is enrolling in the program sees the pictures hanging there of our more than 120 graduating classes (so far). Photos displaying the smiling—no, beaming—faces of every dedicated individual who went through our training, passed class after class, did all the work, stuck with it, and turned their lives completely around. They went from no respect (for themselves and anyone else) and low self-esteem to very high respect for themselves and others, and they cultivated a healthy self-esteem that keeps them stepping only in the direction of their success. They have become contributing members of a society that makes their life rewarding and fulfilling. Each person on The Wall has a story about breaking through limitations, overcoming stereotypes, rising above unhealthy and long-established family systems, and fighting through years of personal rejection. The Wall is a very real testimony to the power of heart, the power of getting beyond the *no* that is dumped daily on our psyches. It is a testimony of what is possible after finding your *Yes*.

Second Chance is successful because our clients are successful. That's the real proof. That's why we are in business, and that's why we have remained in business, growing through the years and helping more and more people who choose to get help. We have done the research, compared a wide variety of programs and systems, selected and combined only what we felt was the best. We have been down the road ourselves, and we know what works and what doesn't. But programs can only go so far.

The Person within the Package

The true reason for our success, the foundation that all else is built upon, the vision shared by each member on our board of directors, and the dedication of our staff is the recognition that, "There but for the grace of God, go I." Without a doubt, our success is due to the underlying respect all of us have for each other and the men and women we serve. Throughout Second Chance, actually throughout my life, respect has been my number one tenet. Respect and integrity go hand in hand.

I had not given the idea of respect much thought until I received the following letter that had been sent to a mutual friend.

> *Dear —,*
>
> *Today I had an amazing experience with a man who has dedicated his life to serving a community that is so often neglected—ex-convicts, the homeless, welfare recipients.*
>
> *While we were sitting outside on a beautiful afternoon at a café, sharing coffee and ideas, an obviously distressed, homeless man came by. He hovered near our table. His face was a patchwork of new stitches—probably 200 stitches crisscrossed his nose and face. It was frightening; I gave him a sideways glance and hoped he would move on.*
>
> *Scott, purposely stopped our conversation and studied the man's face. He then said, "Excuse me, are we sitting at your table?" The man thought for a moment and said, "Well, yes."*
>
> *Scott asked, "Would you like us to move?"*
>
> *The homeless man, summoning the finest of social graces, shook his head as if to say, "Oh no, please don't be bothered on my account."*
>
> *But Scott insisted and said, "We can move. I can tell this is your table. It looks better on you than it does on us."*
>
> *As we picked up our things and moved to*

another table, the man sat in our former spot, which was tucked into a cozy corner of the café patio. He was obviously relieved to be in his comfortable niche.

He turned to me and said, "Thank you. Thank you very much. I really appreciate it." And this man, who otherwise would have been someone whose existence I tried to deny, suddenly flourished into a dignified human being as the filters that obscured my vision melted away.

Scott's ability to immediately sense this man's needs and to offer him the same human dignity I would offer a well-dressed executive provided an immediate transformation for me. This is more than a skill that Scott has honed for fifteen years as the Director of Second Chance. This is an innate "knowing" that has been born out of his willingness to meet his own "darkness" head on. By embracing the darkness in every one of his "clients," he has been able to see past their self-limiting beliefs to the inner success that is waiting to be ignited.

It was humbling to witness this skill at work. Through his commitment, Scott has helped thousands of people who otherwise would have been left to repeat their destructive cycle, flourish into productive, happy, healthy, contributing members of society.

All the best,

My motto, *"Tell Me No. I Dare You!"* is rooted in the belief that each and every individual on the planet has a piece of success tucked into their heart or soul or gut. It is there; it is real; and it is the part of the person that yearns for something good. I have yet to meet the person who does not have at least a speck of that yearning. And I respect the yearning. I respect the person within the package.

This respect is what takes *"Tell Me No. I Dare You!"* from belligerence to a place of certainty that my *Yes* and the *Yes* of some unwashed, bad-smelling, homeless guy come from the same place. It is my task to find that place, make that connection, and respect it. That means I don't say to myself, "What a wreck of a human being! I am better than this wreck." My passion is to help this drugged out, desperate derelict discover clean clothes, clear thoughts, and self-respect. I have been blessed to know this partnership many times over. I am reminded of these blessings every time I walk past The Wall. I hope one day you will come and visit it and see for yourself. I love visitors.

At Second Chance, we have developed specific procedures that many people regard as virtually miraculous. Behind the procedure are five basic transformative principles that will work, not just for those in crisis, they will work for everyone. They will work for you and for those you love, too!

CHAPTER 2

See Scott Run

Today, I help people change their lives from *no* to *Yes*, hard core *no*-sayers, the kind of people you might not want to meet. It wasn't always this way. For many years, I, too, lived a life of *no*. I drank until I passed out or blacked out. I used cocaine and other drugs daily. I sold hashish in Amsterdam. I hid from the world and from myself, becoming a master at it. I hid my using. I hid my thoughts. I hid my hopes and dreams—I hid them for so long that they had learned to hide themselves from me. All that hiding resulted in more craving, more using, more hiding…and a lot of self-hatred. I drifted, by choice, into a life that was spiraling deeper and deeper into negativity and rage.

I started out as a normal kid, though my mother has told me I was always something of a rebel who lived at the very center of his life. No one could ever tell Scott Harris Silverman what to do, not ever. Not even when to be born. The story goes that I was supposed to be born on a Thursday. My mother went to the hospital that night. However, no one told me what the schedule was. My mother went back to the hospital again on Friday night. On Saturday morning, my father and the doctor went to get haircuts while she waited in the hospital for me to decide to be born. Even as an infant, I wanted to be the one in control.

I wasn't born into *no*. Like most kids, I was born into a

magical world ready to say *Yes* at every opportunity. As a child I was free to explore, practice with my bow and arrow, and follow my neighbor as he taught me to use my hands to build and repair. I could walk with my grandfather and our old dog, feeling the love and respect that I had been born into. I lived a life of *Yes* without having to make any conscious thoughts or decisions about it.

My parents were in the retail clothing industry. My mother worked outside the home with my father in the family business. Mothers who work outside the home may be common today, but in the 1950s it was not the norm, at least not in my neighborhood. It gave me the opportunity to say "yes" to the boy I was. We had a housekeeper who could not keep up with me, so I was free to explore my own imagination and sense of adventure. I knew I was loved, and I was blessed with the ability to structure most of my time, basking in the knowledge that I was free.

My mother and father brought my three siblings and me into the family business even before we entered school. They paid us for sorting hangers, putting tags on clothing, wrapping gifts, and going on deliveries. As we grew older, they brought us more fully into their retail business. My early experience of real work along with the freedom I had at home assured me that I was good at something. I had value.

Then came school.

Today, I might receive treatment for ADD or be put in a special program for students with learning disabilities—but not in the 1950s and early 1960s. Back then, you did only what the teacher said and only what the majority did. I am not and never have been in the majority. The schools did not care how well I could take tags off clothes or count hangers. They never asked me to show them that I could take a radiator grill out of the floor or shoot a bow and arrow. They just wanted me to say "See Dick run" when they called on me. And I couldn't. It wasn't just that

I could not read. I didn't really *care* that I couldn't. I would have much rather been outside walking with my grandpa and our dog, creating my own "See Scott run." I felt squeezed into a mold that didn't fit. By the time I was six years old, I had already come to the conclusion that because I was not in the majority, I must be stupid.

Good at *Something*

My parents were worried. They tried me in different schools. On my first day at one of these schools, I was trying to keep my mind busy while the teacher drained the energy and sucked the air out of the room. Then I heard my name. "Scott Silverman, come up and show us on the map where the Pacific Ocean is." I looked at the map with the colors and the shapes. I knew I had a 50/50 chance of getting it right. I got it wrong. The class erupted into laughter. "What a retard!" "Man, how stupid!" "What kinda school did he go to? The dumb kind!"

I sat back down and vowed never, ever, to let that happen again. I would never allow myself to feel that shame again.

I started learning things the school never intended to teach. I learned to hide. I learned to divert attention by acting out in other ways to discourage teachers from calling on me. And I learned to read just enough to get by. There I was, eight, maybe nine years old, and I had already decided I was a failure. I couldn't succeed. I could no longer trust the *Yes* I was born with.

Too many people do the same thing. They abandon the potential they were born with. They leave behind the who and the what they might become, the potential and the vision, along with their old dolls and toy wagons. Many individuals give up, go along, or come to believe that their dreams and aspirations don't count. I could have done that, too. I could have caved in and believed what I was told. I could have resigned myself to being the failure and a screw up they said I was. But a kernel of my *YES* remained, and unbeknownst to me, it continued to germinate.

The rebel in me could not just give up and die. When I was seventeen, a psychologist told me that I was not good at anything and I might as well "become good at doing nothing." My parents paid this inspirational expert, and I took his words as a challenge. For years, I played those words over and over until they became a mantra in my head. I would find something I was good at doing. I might be stupid and unable to achieve success, but I could do something!

My headstrong unwillingness to accept *no* eventually proved to be one of my strengths. But first it translated into rebellion throughout my childhood, teen years, and early adulthood.

Rebellion for rebellion's sake leads to inner destruction, and eats away at the soul. In my rebellion, I discovered alcohol and drugs. I became very good at drinking. By the time I quit, I was gulping down a fifth of alcohol a day while still working full time. Few knew, since I'd gotten so good at hiding. By the time I quit drugs, I was using cocaine, marijuana, amphetamines, and barbiturates, all to wake me up, keep me going, get me to sleep, and control my growing rage. I became so focused on the *no's* of my life that I could not, would not, see the potential for good that was all around me. Something had to give.

My Wake-up Call

By November 1984. I was drinking to the point of blackout on a regular basis. I was in New York City on a buying trip for my parent's retail business. My parents still didn't know how bad my drinking and drugging had gotten. No one did. Not even I knew. My wife, Michelle, and the psychiatrist I was seeing realized that the problem was out of control, yet even they had no idea of the extent of my use.

On November 9, 1984, my rage erupted in a bar in Manhattan.

I had a blackout and got into a brawl. The cops were called, and the Universe stepped in. I should have gone to jail. As luck or God would have it, there was a convention of undercover police officers going on that same week. Because of my family's business in retail and my position of handling certain stores, I carried a silver and gold corporate security badge that identified me in case one of the family stores had a break in or the alarm went off. Guess what color undercover cop badges were?

During the brawl I got tossed outside, where I passed out in the street. The cops came. They looked at the badge. It was dark; they were busy; they probably mistook me for an undercover officer in New York for the convention. I still don't know. What I do know is that New York's finest took me back to my hotel. I passed Go, no jail.

That was my turning point. At that moment, I saw that I could not go on drugging and drinking and drinking and drugging and foisting this fake Scott off on my parents, sisters, brother, and co-workers. The *no* I was living in had taken me to the brink. When you live in the land of *no,* there are no options, there is no potential; there is only a very dead end. A very dead and complete end. I decided I had nothing left to live for.

The next day, November 10, began the way all of my days began. I snorted cocaine in the morning to get me through until I could douse my brain in alcohol. This was normal for me; I would drink until I passed out or blacked out, then I would use coke to get me going for the day ahead. I was in a co-worker's office on the forty-fourth floor of a New York skyscraper. The window was open, and I was alone. It hit me that there was an easier way. All I had to do was sit down on that ledge, lean back, and no more pretending, no more rage, no more no.

Suicide is the ultimate *NO!* It bellows, "Life is not for living! Life is for dodging, for avoiding. Get out while you can!" Suicide does not believe in *Yes* or the hopes and dreams of tomorrow.

Suicide does not believe in faith or love or the beautiful brunette named Michelle who had been married to me for two years and had loved me for far longer. Nope, suicide believes only in *no,* as in *no hope, no good, no tomorrow.*

I took my place, ready to drop to a quick and final end. I felt the cool November air and began to lean back. " Get the hell away from that window before you fall, you idiot!" My associate's words pulled me back into the room. And they pulled me back into life.

As if I'd been tapped on the shoulder just then, I had the first flash of *Yes* I'd had in a long time. I realized something obvious then that I hadn't considered before. *It was okay to ask for help.* I gave myself permission to say "yes" to someone who believed I could get out of the cage where I had locked myself. That someone was Scott! *Yes* became the key I used to open the cell.

Some people give up as they live out their *no's.* Depression and hopelessness kill them from the inside out. Deep within me lay a rage that could have fueled the entire eastern seaboard. It led me to lash out, to drink, to use and abuse drugs. Yet, way down deep inside, I knew that what I believed and what I was doing were wrong, and it angered the hell out of me. I know today that what caused the anger was living my life as a *no. No* goes against all that we are and all that we are born to become. I was lucky and used that anger instead of giving up or giving in. I believe a Higher Power stepped in, calling me to choose a life of *Yes* just as I was ready to end it all in a jump.

Thanks to the power of my brush with death on that November day in 1984, I took a chance on *Yes.* I used it to reach out for help. Here I am, twenty-five years later, with a multi-million-dollar nonprofit agency that I started, a house in Southern California, and a bucket load of trophies and awards. The beautiful brunette still loves me, and to prove it she gave me two other ravishing beauties who adore me. My daughters are young women, and they have become two of the biggest reasons I have for saying "*Yes.*" Recently, CNN filmed me and what I do on one of its segments they call "Hero of the Week." The City of San Diego named February 19, 2008, Scott H. Silverman Day. I share this with you not to brag, but to show you that focusing on *Yes* can change your life in big and small ways, just as it changed mine. *Yes* works.

The Cop-out of Settling

Today, a good friend and the director of development at Second Chance, says, "You can never say no to Scott Silverman."

This surprises some people, but what surprises me is that so many people do take *no* for an answer. I am amazed that people accept what they don't want. They settle for less. Much less.

As a nation, we settle for a 70% recidivism rate for those we let out of prison. That means for every ten people we release from prison, seven will return. Of those ten who went to prison, six will have children who also enter prison, and those children will be released only to reenter and have their children incarcerated in turn.

This sounds crazy, but it is what we do in California and what most states do. Do you have any idea of what this costs? The financial cost of housing *one* person in the California prison system is $44,000 a year! If a car costs $44,000 and there is a 70% chance it will break down, would you buy it? If you went to a doctor who had a 70% death rate among his patients, how long would you stay? What if 70% of jet liners crashed and no one did anything to correct the problem? Would you accept the answer, "No, there's nothing to be done?"

Perhaps you would if you believed it was less trouble to accept that "what is, just is" or you were taught not to make waves. But it is the wave-makers, the people who refuse to take *no* for an answer, who change history. It is wave-makers like Rosa Parks, who would not accept that because of her race she must sit in the back of the bus. She, and others like her, brought all of us to a higher level of integrity and behavior. People united in the cause of freedom show us that every *no* that oppresses is wrong! One mother who refused to stand back and allow any more children to be killed by drunk drivers began MothersAgainst Drunk Drivers. MADD now has over three million members and supporters worldwide. It has only taken twenty-eight years to reach this number and enable MADD to become instrumental in changing the laws about drunk driving. Just imagine, if the courts had said, "Nothing can really be done" about drunk drivers!

Five Keys to Yes

Every day, I encounter some form of *no*. The *no* may come from an ex-felon, or a Second Chance contributor, or perhaps from my board. Sometimes I am even tempted to hear the small *no* in my own head. I don't accept those *no's*, because I understand that if I did, my life would no longer be my own. But, "just saying 'no'" to *no* is not enough. I wish I had learned when I was younger that in order to move from *no* to *Yes,* I needed to say "yes" to *Yes.* To do that, I needed to understand five powerful keys. I'll list them here, then we'll look at each one in depth.

The first key to Yes is to "know your Yes." You can get to *Yes* only if you know what you want to say *Yes* to. If you have no idea of what your *Yes* is, you are, in effect, saying "no" to yourself and the world. Learn to mine your passions to find your *Yes.* Your vision of *Yes* can shield you from merely reacting and jumping back into *no* if or when things don't immediately go the way you want them to. *Yes* is power. We'll explore these dynamics in chapter three.

The second key to Yes is commitment. I needed to make a commitment to get off drugs and alcohol, and that commitment had to be more compelling than my commitment to use them. I needed to find a reason not to use. I found that in my commitment to others. It sustained me and gave me a vision of a *Yes* future. In chapter four we'll discuss how to support your *Yes* to empower your commitment.

The third key to Yes is willingness and courage to open up, change, and get out of your comfort zone. For some people it seems easier to stay comfortable, to settle and accept something unacceptable. To stay comfortable in that way is to cling to *no*. It can be scary to get out of your comfort zone. But, what good is staying comfortable if your comfort zone is deep in *no* and sabotages your whole life? Stretching, reaching, trying something you have never done before may be scary, but it's exciting, and I promise you the rewards far outweigh the temporary discomfort. It's like exercising—you may want to sleep an hour later instead of saying "yes" to exercise, but in five or ten months, you'll be a lot more uncomfortable if you don't go for the run. We'll explore the dangers of the comfort zone and the empowering rewards of getting out in chapters five, six, and seven .

The fourth key to Yes is time. You know your *Yes*. You have committed 100% to do what it takes. You are able to push past the discomfort. You must now take the time to manifest *Yes*. Acorns don't turn into oak trees overnight. *Yes* takes as long as it takes. Shortcuts might work on the drive to Grandma's, but if you want lasting change, you must discover the power in a proactive journey through time. Chapter eight seeks to inspire you in this direction.

The fifth key to Yes is perseverance; there is always a way. People ask me, "What happens when you run out of people to call or run out ideas about how to get your project completed?" My answer is always the same: there is *always* another person to call or re-call and ideas are limitless. This is my unshakable belief. If I believed I would run out of people or ideas, I might quit. I don't quit, however, because I know that there is always a way. Always. The next phone call might be the one I'm waiting for, and the next idea may be the epiphany I'm seeking. The only way to miss out is to stop trying. *There is always a way.* This is so important that chapter nine will inspire you with many examples.

The Game

My life has been a miraculous journey from *no* to *Yes.* I have met many wonderful people who have discovered or learned the keys to *Yes* and used them for their own betterment. The next person I write about could be you. If even one person is able to change, everyone is able to change. If one person can find inner greatness, everyone can find inner greatness.

The saying in Alcoholics Anonymous, "Fake it till you make it," is also true for going from *no* to *Yes.* My hope is that you will read this book and be touched by what I have done in my life, and that you will use the five keys to find your own *Yes. Yes* has now become my drug of choice. It drives me. It juices me. I see it in others, and I find tremendous fulfillment in helping others find it.

We were each sent into this world as a little bundle of pure potential, pure possibility. We were all born as God's *Yes.* Our potential will never evaporate. Our possibility will never be lost. We were born into *Yes,* and that birthright is always there for us to embrace.

Is it a fight to get beyond *no,* to change *no?* Is it is a battle to find a way to *Yes* and to winning? Perhaps. I see it more as a game. How do I get from where I am to where I want to be?

Some people believe that *Yes* requires more time and effort than *no*. It may require more time and more effort, but in the end the rewards are great! Join me in playing this wonderful *Tell Me No. I Dare You!* game. It's a game you can play for the rest of your life. Starting now!

CHAPTER 3

Know Your *YES*

Keeping that first fragile spark of *Yes* alive is never more challenging than at the very beginning. Sweating on the edge of the window ledge in New York, one breath away from suicide, I had reached my "bottom out" moment, the *Yes* spark my only tether to life. When I came in from that ledge, I immediately phoned Michelle.

"Call Grant," I managed to say.

Grant was my shrink. During one session, he had explained to Michelle and me that I needed to get to the end of my rope, hit the bottom, hit a wall, all euphemisms for reaching a place where I had nowhere to go but up or out. The rubber band had to be stretched to its breaking point, until it could stretch no more and do nothing but snap and be left useless – or snap back.

"The rubber band has snapped," I told her.

In 1984, I was thirty years old and, frankly, the idea of taking responsibility for my own life scared the hell out of me. I had no idea where to start. I didn't know what I was going to do, but I agreed to enter rehab. With nothing left to lose, I stopped running from responsibility and gave up playing the "I can fool you" game. I surrendered body, mind, and spirit. Totally surrendered. It was the hardest, easiest, and most courageous thing I had ever done. Anyone who has gone through their own bottom moment knows what I mean. It was hard because I was admitting I couldn't go on. I couldn't play the game any longer. I couldn't bluff my way out of my problems. It was easy because I had to do nothing. I gave up all control. My life was no longer in my hands. It was in the hands of everyone and anyone else. I simply gave up. Eventually, I agreed to put my life in God's hands. And, it was courageous because it was the most responsible choice I'd ever made. It felt almost that safe.

When I look back on my life before 1984, I'm amazed I survived. I was a mess. There was so much I did not know. I was thirty years old and I did not know that I did not know…

…how to drive a car without being under the influence of something. I "knew" substances made me relax, made me alert, and put me in a better place. No one could convince me otherwise. I just knew it.

…how to engage in any social situation without the "benefit" of at least three or four drinks. The booze would loosen me up and make me comfortable, prime me to be the lovable clown, and make me likable. I *knew* I could fool everyone out of seeing the scared, incapable Scott. I knew that drinks made social situations social.

… how to be honest with anyone, especially myself. I knew I could fool everyone, even me, and I could get everyone to like the funny, outrageous me so much that they wouldn't see how insecure I really was. I just *knew* I could fool everyone.

… how to feel true emotion. I had no idea what those words even meant. I knew feeling emotions meant pain and hurt, and I did not want to go there. I knew I wanted to avoid pain and hurt. I *knew* I was good at that!

… how to function while staying clean and sober. I knew life felt better when I was high or drunk. I knew I liked the numbness when the world was a blur. I knew I could get the laughs and attention I craved by being outrageously messed up. All this I knew because all the events of my life *proved* it was true.

All this created layers of self-loathing, and the only *Yes* I could find in my first days of sobriety was "do it for others." I cared about important people in my life more than about myself. I don't believe I would have been successful back then if I had tried to do it just for me. I confess that even now, a small part of me doesn't quite believe I deserve *Yes*. I continue to work on changing that. Thankfully, I now recognize it and understand that life will always be about change. Today, "do it for others" is still my *Yes*, born out of intense love and gratitude. I realize that others—especially non-addicts—are able to find a *Yes* within themselves that is based in self-worth, but if you can't quite get all the way there, you can make your loved ones the basis of your *Yes*. I suppose this goes against a lot of psychology, but when you're desperate for something to work in your life, keeping your spark alive may require this connection.

Remodeling My House

Rehab lasted thirty days. I checked in, and I stayed. Rehab was a lot like remodeling a house. You've got a lot of trash to throw out before you can begin putting up new walls or installing new fixtures. You have to rip things out, tear things away, and sometimes blow up the old structures. I had a lot of structures that needed to be tossed out, like the lies I had told myself so often that I believed them. I had the suppliers and liars I had kept as friends. I had the habits that held me down. I had the *no* blinders that kept me from seeing and hearing clearly.

I spent the first few days in detox, where years and years of toxins were literally forced out of my cells. All the poisons I had accumulated were being power-flushed out of my body, and it was excruciating. And that's just physically.

Emotionally, it was even tougher.

My thoughts were shrouded in deep layers of what felt like heavy, damp wool. I was often cold. Shivering cold. My thoughts pressed on me like horrible vice grips that squeezed my head and would not let go. That time for me was unimaginably and endlessly miserable. Nevertheless, I persevered, because as dark as those days were, and as empty as my life had become, I still had my *Yes*.

I told myself over and over again, "This will be over and you will feel better. You have felt worse. Every day you are moving closer to sobriety." And I believed it! It was as if I was in a place with no light, but I continued to sense that small laser speck in the distance. I knew if I kept my focus on that light, I would reach it. This was a strong vision for me all during rehab. As long as I could see the speck of light, I had a chance. That speck of light was a miracle to me. It was the difference between a sliver of hope and no hope at all. Without that light, there would have been no way out. You have to just feel that it is there and turn toward it. This part is impossible to explain any more clearly, but I believe it's in all of us and there for us to access.

That little speck of light kept me going. Without it, everything in my world would have disintegrated. Without a doubt, I would not be writing these words today, helping beautiful people, or doing what I can to make a difference in the world. I was put here with things to do. Someone is counting on me. I am driven today because I know how many people are counting on me. And I now embrace the responsibility to be a difference-maker. All because of that little speck of light.

Eventually, the food stayed down and the medications allowed me to manage the shakes. I could see results, and I knew I was getting better. Because of my physical improvement, I thought the rest of rehab would be downhill. But, it turned out that detox was just the beginning of my learning.

Shut up and Listen

Rehab had another dimension: group. I might have been over the detox hump, but now I had to go to group meetings: education groups, AA groups, emotional groups, and family groups. One of the rules of rehab was that everyone was supposed to attend these meetings. Someone else made this rule up, and for the first time in a long time, I followed someone else's rule. I showed up at every single meeting, day after day. I could have stayed in bed or watched TV and loafed, as I'm sure others did. But I didn't. I showed up, and I worked. I worked harder than I had ever worked in my life. I resolved to pay attention. *Yes* was that important to me. My own rules had almost destroyed me. I was ready to try something new.

Group proved to be a miraculous learning ground. It was as sobering an experience as I could imagine. I was not coddled and caressed. I was not pitied. My shortcomings were not excused. Quite the opposite. I was challenged to become responsible for taking the first steps away from *no*.

In her song, *Rehab,* Amy Winehouse sings, "...nothing you can teach me that I can't learn from Mr. Hathaway." Another line in her song is, "...nothing they done taught me did I know." I don't know what rehab Amy Winehouse went to, but it wasn't mine. I may not have known I was addicted, but I learned I was. I learned the only way *out* was *through*. I learned that I could deal with life only on life's terms. I learned I needed help, and I learned to ask for help. I learned to stop blaming life, teachers, and my brain. I learned to take responsibility for myself and my problems. I learned so much. I learned because I chose to.

At one point early in my in-patient rehab, I was given a drug named Risperdal, a medication typically prescribed for autism, schizophrenia, and bi-polar disorder, to help with my detox, my thinking, and my low-level depression. I took it because I was told to take it. Unfortunately, it made me feel as if I was floating.

I was spacey and dopey and not able to pay much attention.

While I was on this drug, a group leader asked, "Do any newcomers have questions?" Under the influence of Risperdal, what I heard was, "Do…an….newcums…quests?" I sat there, staring, and finally spoke up. The best question I could come up with was, "How does this program work?" I was asking a serious question because I was seriously interested in the answer, and besides, nothing else I heard was making any sense.

"Just take the cotton out of your ears and stick it in your mouth." That was my warm and fuzzy welcome to Group 101. I asked another question. I can't even remember what that question was. It was the answer I got from an AA member that was important." Shut the f*** up and listen." That may have been the best advice I have ever heard in my life.

I had to learn to shut my mouth and listen. It is easy to do all the talking, to not pay attention, or to figure out what you're going to say next while someone else is talking. So many of us wait to talk rather than listen.

It is easy to go through life never paying attention to people who aren't saying something you absolutely want to hear. For so many years, I heard only what I wanted to hear, what I thought would lead me to fun and excitement. I wasn't hearing, and I wasn't listening. If I wanted to turn my life around, I had to learn to how to listen, really listen. I learned that if I didn't take the time to listen and connect, I would spend my day reacting, not leading. Reaction brings only pain. Pain for me. Pain for you. Pain for others. In merely reacting I was dedicating my life to all the dead-end compulsions and automatic behaviors that had made *no* so familiar in the first place. Conscious listening is a pathway to *Yes*. It enabled me to find true personal power in choosing and leading my own direction. My AA introduction may have been coarse, but it was right, and I heard it. I finally heard *Yes!*

Yes Is Everywhere

During the hours I was not in group, I had a lot of time to think and to feel so very grateful. I realized I had been given a second chance and that chance was, in the simplest terms, to pursue a life filled with *Yes*. I was ready and willing to follow the directions of others. My old way of thinking and living, of saying "no" to possibility and potential, had landed me in rehab. I was bright enough, or desperate enough, to look for a *Yes* and to listen when the *Yes* arrived, without regard for where it came from.

A man named Bill W. once said, *Yes, it is possible* to break the chains of addiction. Because this one man refused to heed the doubters who proclaimed that addiction could not be defeated, millions of men and women now have lives of sobriety. The twelve-step program he created for Alcoholics Anonymous has saved lives, prevented pain, and averted sadness for millions of people around the world.

I began seeing the power of *Yes* everywhere. In 1954, the track world "knew" that man was not capable of running a mile in less than four minutes. Sir Roger Bannister refused to listen to the nay-sayers who said it was impossible. Instead, he heard, *Yes, it is possible.* He broke the four-minute mile on May 6, 1954. His *Yes* shattered the limiting track mythology, and within two months, John Landy had also broken 4-minute barrier. Today, in 2009, the mile record holder is Hicham El Guerrouj of Morocco, who ran a 3:43.13 mile in 1999. Someone, somewhere, is hearing the words, "Yes, it is possible to beat the current record." And someone, somewhere, will.

Breast cancer activists have heard their *Yes*. It expresses itself in three-day marches, special stamps, and famous pink ribbons. Every day, you see reminders that millions of people believe we can bring an end to this deadly disease. Their passion and light and their worthy cause have drawn people and support like a magnet draws iron. They refuse to hear the *no* when it says "You'll never beat cancer." It is only a matter of time until the passion and commitment of individuals, families, and communities saying *Yes* truly does find a cure for this disease.

Inspiration, motivation, and *Yes* abound, especially when you are looking for them.

Many people don't know how or where to look or what to listen for. Some look in the wrong places, places where *Yes* can't be found. They hear the wrong messages or hear only the *no*.

Some turn to gangs, where they think they can find acceptance and a sense of belonging. But gangs are no substitutes for family and no places to find *Yes*. Others turn to drugs, which offer escape, instant results, and a false sense of security. But drugs are like the Siren in the Odyssey, luring even the bravest sailors to certain destruction on the rocks. Still others turn to crime, hoping to solve urgent, immediate problems but creating bigger, long-term ones and trapping themselves in a *no*-oriented way of life. Some people use their past and their hard luck as excuses for holding them back or keeping them down. From the dramatic to the mundane, people sabotage themselves with *no* and all the excuses that accompany it.

Finding Your *Yes*

Even when you think you've been dealt a bad hand, it is always possible to find *yes*. But you have to look and listen for it. And you have to be ready to accept it. Don't wait for *Yes to* find you. You may be waiting a long time. *Yes* is a birthright, but it's not a destiny. At least, not yet. Thousands of people find it every year. Thousands! They find it because they *choose* to find it.

How do they find it? They look for it, and they *listen* for it. When you listen, you'll hear what you listen for: If you want to hear *No*, that's what you'll hear; if you want to hear *Yes*, you'll hear that instead. And when you hear *Yes*, you have to be open to embracing it.

People can find solutions for their personal obstacles as soon as they find their *Yes*. As I grew past my addictions, my insecurities, and my *no*, I began to get very excited about the possibilities of *Yes*. I began to see not just what *Yes* could do for me, but what it meant to the bigger scheme of things. When neighborhoods and communities come together and identify their common *yes*, they can work together to solve their common problems. When groups of people find their yes, they can share resources and pool time and talent to help their struggling and troubled members and give hope and direction to those who need it. When nations find a global *Yes*, they can solve the tragic problems faced by the needy and underprivileged everywhere. Amazing things can be accomplished when people discover *Yes*. I didn't know exactly what I was going to do with this stunning appreciation for the possibilities of *Yes*, but it became part of my passion and my vision.

How can you access your *Yes*?

- Reach for that place of *knowing* inside that feels like your spark; ask for guidance in finding it, if necessary; focus on it. Listen consciously. *Yes* reverberates loudly when you listen for it

- Instead of merely reacting, choose your own direction

- Pay attention when you feel a passionate connection; you're building your *Yes*

- Look for the *Yes* everywhere

And once you begin listening for *Yes*, you'll be ready for the next step: committing yourself to embracing change.

CHAPTER 4

Commitment

As much as I love the word *Yes,* I have always felt uncomfortable with its sister word, "commitment." Today, I may be one of the most committed individuals you'll ever meet, yet I have never liked the word itself. Commitment sounds narrow, and I am all about expansion. So in order to accept the need for commitment in my life, I had to learn the paradoxical wisdom that in order to expand, I needed to narrow myself. I still don't like the word because of its boundary-setting, but I accept how critical it is to recovery and goal-setting. Thus, a rigorous understanding of what goes into commitment is helpful.

Every person on the planet has commitments, of course. The question is, to what are they committed? And, do their actions support that commitment?

If you look at the lives people lead, you will be able to answer that question. Do they spend time exercising and eating foods that build and not destroy? Do they abstain from harmful drugs and abusive amounts of alcohol? Do they get enough sleep? If the answer is yes, they are more than likely committed to health. Do people you know swear they are committed to education and yet continually vote "no" on bond referendums and never visit a library? Their commitment does not match their actions.

Focusing and Acting

For a commitment to move you forward, it is absolutely essential that you focus and act on what you say you believe. For example, if you say you are committed to your marriage and doing all that you are able to do to make your wife happy, but then ignore her night after night, forget important dates, and generally take her for granted, you are lying. When our government states it is committed to drug reform and then allocates little or no support to programs that are successful, I question their stated commitment. Positive commitment often demands unselfishness; it often begets the need to stretch and grow; it often takes us outside our comfort zone. Positive commitment is seldom easy.

Once I finished rehab, I spent my first year of sobriety becoming acquainted with commitment. How would commitment change my life? Could I stay committed to sobriety if I had to give up my friends? Could I stay committed to my potential if I had to give up my job in our family business? Could I stay committed to my newfound *Yes* if I had to completely rework my entire life? I was determined to answer "yes" to each of these questions.

I had always been able to make the easy commitments, remaining unfocused, reacting instead of taking action. When Michelle and I married in 1982, I was a committed drug and alcohol user. I demonstrated my commitment to the high life by giving each of my groomsmen a flask filled with alcohol and, in the Rabbi's chamber, treating them to rails of cocaine before the ceremony. I sweated through the ceremony not because I was nervous, but because the cocaine made me perspire. As the Rabbi spoke ancient words that would bind us until death did us part, I committed myself to getting a drink once the ceremony was over.

Contrast that to my commitment during my first year of sobriety. I focused on doing what needed to be done to move myself forward, no matter what it took. For many people, recovery can be very tough during the first year and relapse always lurks just around the corner. I was so desperate to save my life, my marriage, and my future that my commitment to stay with the program never faltered. I did what the program told me to do.

Breaking Old Patterns

A team of people at the recovery center met together and chose the best actions for each us in rehab to take in order to achieve lasting recovery. They asked me about my lifestyle when I worked in the business. I told them that the stress was high, the hours long, and it was easy to justify and then hide my addictions. They told me I had to leave the family business.

It was a difficult decision for me to accept. But I could now realize that I had to do it. It had been too easy for me to find people to party with and even easier to fool my parents about what I was doing. It was the perfect life for an addict. When I asked, "Will this bring me sobriety?" The obvious answer was *no*. I knew it was a life I could no longer afford.

Such a drastic change made me nervous, and I wasn't sure how my family would react. It sounds simple enough, but there were complications. Besides, I liked many aspects of the business: the people, the travel, and the regular paycheck. I had no other business to go to and was trained for nothing else. I had been married only two years, and now I was being told to let go of the means to support my wife. I had to make a difficult, conscious choice.

Choosing

Commitment always asks that we move toward whatever we say we are devoted to doing and away from and past whatever gets in the way. It's true that my *Yes* meant that I was getting sober for others, so this decision weighed on me heavily. My parents had started the business thirty-four years earlier. Not only was I being asked to leave a secure future, but choosing to leave would mean as much disappointment for my father and mother as it meant for me. I would be walking away from the dream my parents had nurtured since before I was born. From the time I was a small child, I had always heard, "Someday, all of this will be yours."

Dad's dream had always been to own retail shops. In college, he focused all of his attention on this dream, and in 1950, he had the opportunity to make it a reality. He and my mother took what money they received in wedding gifts and borrowed some more from my grandparents to buy a store and merchandise in El Cajon, California. My father couldn't afford to give up his traveling salesman job until the store showed a profit. So, my mother stepped in and committed to selling all the merchandise they had purchased. She lived in a motel in El Cajon in 1950 and took a six-mile bus trip each way, on her own, to the store. In the evening, she sat at the table in the small motel and hand-lettered the tags and tickets that she'd attach to the merchandise the next day. When the business needed to replenish the inventory, she went to the market and bought more. She was twenty-three and she had no retail experience, but she knew that this venture was their future, and to that she was committed without question. Once my father was able to quit his sales job and give his full attention to the retail business, he and my mother opened a second and then a third store. They worked side-by-side to build a business their children could step into.

I hated disappointing them, but I was committed to getting sober. I loved being in a family business, yet I never actually liked working in retail. My *Yes* couldn't find a true home there, and keeping my *Yes* alive was the only thing that would save me. So for me the right choice was obvious: I had to leave.

Their dream of a passing their business down to generation after generation died when I chose to step away, but they were more committed to me and my recovery than they were to the dream they had clung to for more than three decades. Dreams are powerful things, but sometimes recovery means letting go of someone else's dream to make room for your own. From the time I entered rehab, my question was always, "Will this bring me sobriety?" It was as simple as that.

My parents gave me their blessings without complaint. I am truly lucky to have a family that models commitment. I resigned from the business, and, surprisingly, I actually grew closer to my family.

Getting Support

I had one major advantage over many recovering addicts: my wife and family. The greater your support system, the greater the likelihood of sticking with your *Yes*. My first year of recovery was stress free. Michelle was working and her paycheck helped cover expenses. I focused on sobriety and changing the ways of thinking that had brought me to the bottom. I dedicated myself to lasting recovery. Michelle dedicated herself to me.

In trying to facilitate your recovery, other well-meaning entities may sabotage your *Yes*. In 1984, addiction was considered a disease in California, and addicted individuals were eligible to apply for disability. To do that, California law required that the person applying must also be tested for employment skills. I was tested and told I should pursue welding. I hadn't yet focused the passion I was feeling about life and helping others, but welding seemed more likely than retail to enable a *no* lifestyle. It didn't make a lot of sense to a person who had spent his life in the retail clothing industry. I knew buying, selling, inventory, shipments. I knew profit and loss, hiring and firing, and distribution. But welding? The only experience I had with welding was the brief time I was high on coke and made metal art, sniffing the fumes. I decided they must have mixed up the tests and elected, instead, to take a month and contemplate what I could do. The month turned into a year.

Prayer became a vital part of my support during my recovery, but my rehab team had encouraged a different kind of prayer than what I was used to. My day would begin with prayer, down-on-my-knees prayer, as instructed. Now, I am Jewish, and Jewish people do not pray on their knees. This is what other religions do. I had been brought up to be a good Jewish boy and then a good Jewish man. I did not pray on my knees. It went against all that I knew and believed. I had no idea how I was going to make this happen! A buddy told me, "Scott, when you go to bed, put your cigarettes under the bed. When you wake up you will have to get on your knees to locate your smokes. Say a prayer while you are down there." Good advice. That'll sure fool God! (I stopped smoking a long time ago, but I still pray. Just not on my knees.)

It took a lot for me to drop my act, let go of my ego, and surrender, but I had done that in rehab. Praying on my knees helped remind me that some things were bigger than I was. I kept asking for help in discovering what it was I most wanted, and what I could do that day to keep moving into the light and out of the darkness. I learned I had one basic choice. Each and every day I could choose to follow *Yes* or to follow *no*. Before recovery, I didn't think I had any choice. Actually, I thought very little. I just reacted. My new routine of morning prayer set the day's foundation.

After prayer, I'd kiss Michelle goodbye and go to a group meeting, reinforcing my commitment, an essential form of support. I went to twelve-step meetings and explored my demons, and Michelle would always listen to what I had to say. She also went to Al-Anon to learn how to be even more supportive—and to cope. I never let a day pass that year without attending at least one meeting and sometimes two or three.

Few actions validate recovery more than volunteering. I volunteered every day at Sharp Memorial Hospital, the same hospital that helped me get sober. My next commitment was to give back to those who had helped me and to "pay it forward" to those who could use what I had once needed. Eventually, I had volunteered over 4,000 hours. It is true what the holy books tell you: you get more from giving then you do from taking.

Taking the Time

Taking time to manifest *Yes* is one of my five steps, but I include a small section about it in this commitment section because it was part of the commitment process. The five main steps don't happen in sequence in real life. We're usually working on all of them at once in some form. Time is an important factor in the twelve-step program: committing to sobriety one day at a time—which I did. I just didn't think much about the future.

Taking time allowed me the most important part of my days while I was recovering—and I'm not kidding. This phase of my life prove to be so healing that it was almost magical. It was like floating around in *Yes*. During afternoons, I spent my time flying kites. That's right, flying kites. Stunt kites, or as some people refer to them, acrobatic or sport kites, fly only two to three feet off the ground. The object is to control and maneuver the kite. There are two strings attached to the kite. These two lines are connected to handles on one end and to a type of kite bridle on the other. The kite flyer controls the kite by pulling on one string or the other. If you want to make the kite go right, for example, you pull on the right line. It is pretty easy to learn to fly these kites. Like life, the trick comes in mastering the turns.

I committed to be the best, most knowledgeable kite flyer in San Diego. It may not seem like much, but it was a commitment

I could keep successfully. I ate and drank kites—a new addiction. We went to Hawaii, and I took my kites. Michelle had visions of beach time, sun time, lying in the sand, and holding hands time. Instead, we went shopping for kites—handmade kites, faster kites, kites to have for a long glorious time.

Flying a kite is a great analogy for life. You can turn in any direction you desire, yet it is up to the wind to keep the kite moving. If you lay back and let the wind take over, the chances of the kite crashing go up. If you try to control the kite too tightly, the kite also crashes. The kite operator needs to stay awake, listen to and watch the wind, and then use the wind to his advantage. A small gentle pull moves the kite. If you are too rough, in fact, you have to start again. For probably the first time since childhood, I lived fully in the moment and became one with it. Flying a kite is a coming together of nature and man. When that happens, the results can be spectacular. All I had to do was do my part, and the wind would do its part, just as in life. Show up, do your part, and the Universe will become your partner.

I listened to that inner voice of my heart and found the strength to make the right choices and take the right actions, like leaving the family business. My priorities grew sharper and more compelling. I didn't quite know it then, but some part of my spirit was working on my true calling on those wonderful afternoons outdoors.

Eventually my kite phase ended. Michelle was happy. What I owe Michelle is beyond the scope of repayment. While I was learning about commitment, Michelle was living it.

The Power of Commitment

What would have happened if I had listened to the committee, not trusted my own inner voice, and became a welder? I might have been able to stay sober and I might have been happy enough, but I doubt I would have been fulfilled. During the first year of sobriety, the following acts of commitment set the foundation for my life today:

- Breaking old patterns and making changes
- Maximizing and appreciating support for my commitments
- Listening to my heart's voice, feeling my higher power during prayer and meditation, asking for help
- Getting help through meetings
- Making choices by asking: will this action lead to sobriety? Is this part of my *Yes*?
- Volunteering
- Taking life one day at a time, and allowing time to recreate myself
- Sorting out priorities

These continue to be my commitments. And they bring me so much fulfillment.

During that first year of sobriety, I kept in touch with the *Yes* that was my potential, and I found out what I could truly commit to. My very first commitment was, of course, sobriety. It still is. If I didn't have my sobriety, I had death and absolutely nothing else.

In that first year, I did what people I trusted told me to do. I learned that to be committed means doing whatever it takes to stay committed. I had to let go of my ego and my need to be right. I had to find the courage to face what had landed me in this place of recovery and to admit the destruction and hurt that I had caused. I finally understood that what I do and say and think today affects tomorrow and tomorrow and tomorrow. Commitment was not just an idea; commitment was an action. Commitment was work.

By the end of 1985, I had a new structure in which I could live. I had spent hundreds of hours in prayer and contemplation, deciding what I needed to change (which was pretty much everything) and what I needed to do to empower my new life. My commitment to sobriety, family, helping others, and giving back would be the new walls of my life. The foundation would revive the *Yes* I was given at birth. Everything I did, everything I said, was done inside that framework. It has now been twenty-four years. Some of the walls have been moved and changed, but my foundation has never shifted over those years.

My foundation of *Yes* shaped my commitments, and my commitments reinforced my foundation. My commitments helped me say no to things that deserved a *no* and say yes to things that demanded a *Yes*. It was easy to say no to drugs and alcohol when I could hear the beat of *Yes* in my heart. By committing to my family, it took little effort to say no to people, places, or things that would have taken me away from them. My commitments have grown as I continue to grow.

Commitments narrow my life, which for me seem to go against what I know I want: growth, freedom, and opportunity. I want a big, wide life. The paradox is that by narrowing my options, I have expanded my potential. This is the wisdom I absorbed as I operated that stunt kite twenty-four years ago. It continues to enrich my life and the lives of all those I help today.

I learned that commitment is really about doing what needs to be done. Viewed that way, commitment does not narrow my life. It broadens it. When I know what needs to be done, I have learned to focus on it and then stay the course. Commitment liberates.

I may not like the word, but I do like commitments and their results.

CHAPTER 5

Stop Hiding

Have you ever had something you could call a safety zone? The entire first half of my life, I went searching for a zone just like that—a safe place to hide, a place I could call my own, a place where I could get away from a world in which I did not fit.

Not fitting, or just feeling that way, is probably not all that unusual for lots of kids. There were the cool kids, the sports jocks, the smart book-wormy study-till-you-get-an-A freaks, and the rebels who were in the "Oh yeah? Watch me!" club. And then there were the loners-who-didn't-want-to-be-loners-but-were-loners. They just didn't have a group, or a bunch, or a club. They were outside everything, looking in. That was me. Rebellious? In 1964 that was a word I heard so often I began to believe it was a part of my given name.

Rebellion

I hated school. I suppose I have made that clear as I have been writing, yet I find it almost impossible to describe the actual physical sensations my young body experienced Monday through Friday. Just waking up in the morning triggered the feeling of not enough air to breathe and not enough space. By fourth grade we were able to change rooms for a few classes, and that brought some relief from being forced to constrict a football field of energy into a pint container.

By fourth grade I could read, but I could not sit still. Hell, I still cannot sit or stand still. I'd fidget and twist and drop books and do whatever I could to keep moving. It felt as if I were being suffocated when I sat in my seat and attempted to listen to the drone of whomever was standing at the front of the room. It had nothing to do with a particular teacher, even though there were certain teachers who brought out more fidgeting than others. It was *always* the teacher who most wanted me to or ordered me to be still. The more they would say "Behave, sit still, be quiet, listen, sit down," the more I would do exactly the opposite. Kinda spit in their face, metaphorically speaking. It felt good, like getting my *Yes* back—except that nine-year-olds need positive mentoring, not alienation.

It was on a day with a teacher who *really* demanded I sit and shut up that I decided I would make pinshots and spice up a very boring afternoon. For those of you who were able to sit still, pinshots are made from straight pins. I would find them at home and put them in my pockets as I walked out the door. I would then bend the pin into a very precise 45 degree angle, fashion a miniature slingshot out of a rubber band, and see how many times I could hit the clock at the front of the room. Mr. V. had expressly forbidden the class from making, possessing, or shooting pinshots, but that was a *no*, and at that point in my life, *no* was the switch to turn on my determination.

Ping! Ping! I had four hits to the clock out of six attempts. I was doing pretty well, and Mr. V. was looking frustrated—even better. As I loaded my seventh pinshot into my trusty band, Mr. V. took hold of my arm and had me out of my seat and headed to the hallway before I could beat my record of three hits straight in a row. This was 1964 when children's feelings were not to be considered in matters of insubordination. Mr. V. lit into me, his face so close I could see the few hairs his razor had missed. He threatened and screamed and told me to stay in the hall until he decided if and when I deserved to be allowed back into the class.

Deserved? I hung out in the hallway kicking at dust specks and practicing throwing a nonexistent ball. At some point Mr. V. finally decided I was deserving; he fetched me from the hallway and told me to sit down and shape up. He had no idea that I had been putting together a mini arsenal during my exile. Back in my seat, I quickly loaded my rubber band with pinshots. Ping. Ping. Ping. Six hits dead center on the clock! All within seconds, and all while Mr. V. had his back to the class. He turned around quickly, trying to catch me. He knew I had done it, spit smack in the middle of his face—his veins-throbbing, nostrils-flaring, cheeks-flushing, big, fat face. It was more than a personal record. It was a personal victory! When the bell rang, Mr. V was still sputtering and yelling. His face was so red, it appeared he would soon start bleeding from his eyes. Such power I had!

I was buoyant as I made my way to the next classroom. I took my seat. And then I heard them, in the distance, the sound of sirens getting louder and louder. My first thought was that maybe this was going to be the best day ever: six hits in a row, getting the best of Mr. V., and the school was on fire.

Fear

I could see through the windows that it was not fire trucks, however, but police cars and an ambulance. As all of this was taking place, I was summoned to the office. The principal and I were on very familiar terms. I had spent a great deal of time in his office; he and his secretary knew me well. I strolled into the office with a smile for the secretary and wondered what I had done now. I hoped my parents would not be called.

Alas. My parents had already been called, and I was ordered

to sit. There was something about the atmosphere that got my attention. I grew quiet and still.

"Listen, Mr. Silverman, Mr. V. just had a heart attack. You see all these bright lights around outside? That is *your* doing, young man. You brought that heart attack on just as sure as if you hit him with a rock right in the heart! If he dies, *if he dies*, you little rebel, that will be the end. You will go to jail for manslaughter. That'll teach you. You better hope he makes it, Mr. Troublemaker Silverman. You just better hope he makes it."

I started hoping, wishing, and praying that Mr. V. made it. "Let him be, okay. Please let him live. Please let him live. Please let him live." This became my litany. I have no recollection of how I felt. I think I just went as blank as I have ever been. I'm sure I was terrified. I wasn't yet ten years old. It was 1964. Crimes were punished. Murderers went to prison if they were lucky, or to "the chair" if they weren't.

The idea that they were trying to scare me into behaving or trying to get my parents to take me out of their school (a very well-known private school) never crossed my mind until at least a decade later. There was no adult who said, "Manslaughter? Are they friggin' nuts?" There was no one who even considered the idea that placing such fear in the heart of a nine-year-old might have all sorts of unanticipated negative consequences. I was alone with the fear that a man might die because I had beat my record and had hit the clock *dead center* six times in a row within seconds.

Mr. V. survived.

I threw out my straight pins, my rebellious *Yes* utterly crushed. Fear drove my rebellion underground. But to get through the harsh experience of my early schooling, I needed a safe place. I had to find one.

False Safety

I have no idea how many safe places I discovered for myself as a little kid only to have them infiltrated by some stranger, causing me vivid pain and the exasperating inconvenience of the ordeal. Then, as would happen so often later in life, the adversity drove me to get creative. I decided to make my own safe place.

I loved building, creating, and using my hands. We had a neighbor who let me trail around behind him, watch him, ask questions, and learn. He showed me how to use machines and saws and how to measure and nail without hitting my thumb. I learned all of this before I was ten. So, as a resourceful little kid with plenty of will power, I built myself a fort as high as I could go, about ten or twelve feet up in a big lush pine. Superman had his Fortress of Solitude, and I had mine. I set out to build my fortress, my tree house, completely by myself, for myself. I would have my very own safety zone.

I carefully nailed pieces of wood into the trunk of the giant pine, sweating in the summer heat, and climbed high enough to lay out the base. Piece by piece, I carried and hoisted wood planks and plywood. Time flew by and stood still all at once. I was in my element—busy every day until it was complete. And then, I'd add a little more, and make it better.

My nine-year-old hands became calloused as I learned to take out splinters on my own. Building that tree house took weeks and weeks. Once finished with the "house" part of it, I made a ladder from rope. I tied one end of the rope to the trunk of the tree, just above the floor of my tree house, and the other end hung loose, just about ground level. I tied a big knot in the rope every foot or so, making easy for me to climb up into my fortress. This rope gave me the ultimate in privacy. I could climb into my tree house, pull up the rope, and no one could find me. I was safe.

It was where I went when I failed another test, or my temper had erupted, or I did something that brought out the frowns and looks of disappointment. It's where I went when my heart ached to be good, and I knew I didn't know how. It was where I went when the world became too big for seventy pounds of undirected energy.

Sometimes, actually many times, I gathered the avocados from the neighbors' trees and carried them up to my den. They became torpedoes or missiles I directed at the enemy. Back then, there were a lot of enemies. No one really knew where these avocado bombs were coming from, and if they did find out, they had no way of reaching me.

I loved that tree. The rich fragrance of pine would get into my hands and clothing. I could lie on my back and look through the needles, breathe in the smells, and dream.

My dreams were the dreams of a nine-year-old boy. I could be Matt Dillon from *Gunsmoke* or Davy Crockett, defending my own Alamo. I could be a hero, rescuing others who might be helpless or in trouble. I could save lives and say it was just part of who I am, all in a day's work.

In those dreams of mine, there was never any frustration about the way my written letters would line up on my paper. I never had to hear stupid demands that I do my best. My best was always what I knew how to do and what I loved. My best did not involve books, stuffy rooms, or rules. My best involved only what I was good at, and at those things I always and only did my best, with no demands necessary.

Sometimes the wind would turn my fortress into a ship out on the high seas, like in *Swiss Family Robinson*. I would protect my family and defend my ship from pirates and storms and sea monsters. Regardless of the enemy, I always won. Always.

At times I could be lulled into sleep and awaken only to realize that classrooms, chores, and a world I could not navigate awaited me at the bottom of the rope ladder. I learned that safety was mine to create, and that I was safest when I hid.

Evolving Comfort Zones

As with all comfort zones, I couldn't stay there forever. I had to move on or wither. I couldn't stay a boy, and teenagers didn't hang out in trees. The fear and shame were still locked inside me, though. Fortunately, in seventh grade, I made a friend. We were in shop class together. He was impressed by the fact that I finished my projects before anyone else. I'm not sure if that was what made him seek me out, but seek me out he did, and my life improved.

I had someone to hang out with, invent things with, and plot with. We had some of the same classes, and we were neighbors. Perfect. I've told people that it was Tom who gave me my first joint, but it was probably the other way around. Or it could have been an older girl that Tom and I befriended. Lydia lived down the street. She drove us around, got us beer, and managed to smoke a lot of dope with us.

I had a whole new comfort zone. This was in 1966 and 1967. Very good years. It was a time of rebellion for anyone under the age of thirty, and we were no exception. We'd hang out drinking, doping, listening to ZZ Top or Led Zeppelin, and talking about how screwed up the world was. We never talked about how screwed up *we* were. There was plenty to rebel against; there were all these drugs and all this alcohol, and the rest of the world was the problem. By the time my parents sent me to boarding school, I was past the early stages of addiction.

My mother and father were good, educated Jewish parents who wanted their sons and daughters to grow into good, educated Jewish parents. I was Jewish, but I just couldn't be what the world called good, and I couldn't seem to get myself educated.

Shame

My family prized education, but this was one area where I simply did not fit. It caused my parents a great deal of pain. My own pain took the form of shame, which I covered with anger. I tried to cover the anger with Secanol, alcohol, and marijuana. But over time, my anger prevailed, and my shame only grew deeper.

Shame is not something that lives on the outside of a person. It lives down inside each and every cell and recreates itself as each new cell is formed. Shame wraps you in gunmetal gauze and covers your eyes with the darkest of glasses that direct your sight to the wrongness of your being. Shame tells you, "Something is wrong with *you*, and that something is unspeakable and unfixable. You were created wrong and wrong you shall stay." Shame does not allow for God or good. In shame, there is never a chance for *Yes* because your very being is a *no*.

Some people cover up their shame by trying to be perfect. They are on a noble quest to please everyone by surpassing all expectations so that they will never be discovered as flawed and unacceptable. I never thought of even attempting that route. I gave up little Scottie and his dreams and his desire to fight back when I had my first drink. Why fight back when there was such an easy way to hide and disappear into a handy dandy comfort zone?

Fooling Others

Instead of pursuing a noble quest for perfection, I became the comedian in the spotlight, the entertainer for the evening, whenever I drank. Overnight I became popular. People wanted me around. I was good at something. I could drink! Like other addicts, I could charm.

No one thought I drank too much or too often, especially me. I was young. I could handle it. I was letting off steam. I was working at a job I liked. And I was so good at it! No worries. I'd settle down later. I did not settle down, later or ever. I have never settled down. I no longer drink or drug, but settling down is still not a term I like or use.

My drinking became more focused and purposeful. I would drink before I went out so that I would be ready to party when my friends started to drink. I wanted to be able to entertain right away. I never questioned if what I was doing was normal or if it could be a sign of trouble. I only knew it worked, and so I did it more and more.

My parents finally sent me to a private school in Tucson to get me through the last part of high school. It was a school for dysfunctional boys run by dysfunctional teachers and administrators. I still have memories of one teacher in particular who pulled a gun on a group of us who were acting up. I learned a lot at that school. I'm not sure it is what my parents had planned or hoped I would learn, but I learned. After a series of incidents and accidents, the private school suggested that I would be better served somewhere else, so I returned to San Diego with no direction but with a vast and practical knowledge of marijuana and all the right tools to make a very good drug cocktail.

It's easy to find drug buddies. There is an energy that is sent out and a gravitational pull brings drug, druggie, and buddies together. I would tell my parents that I was off for a camping weekend. I would then hook up with friends who owned motorcycles and scooters.

I should explain here that I had become quite proficient at the art of persuasion and was adept at using it to get almost anything I wanted from my parents, never realizing that in practicing dishonesty to others, I was practicing dishonesty with myself. Even my best nagging had not produced the scooter I wanted, however, and on top of that, I had been forbidden to have a cycle. So, I turned to Plan B: I knew people who had them.

We would ride out to the desert, giddy, with vast amounts of alcohol and even more drugs. Seconal, a very powerful downer, was easy to get. One of the kids I knew during this time had a father or mother who worked in a drug lab. This kid figured out how to sneak into the lab and procure Seconal. He was a popular guy. Marijuana was easier to obtain than alcohol, and there was always someone that could procure some type of hallucinogenic. This was our cocktail, along with cocaine and methamphetamines. Then, as if there were throngs of spectators amazed by our daring, we would ride those bikes directly through a huge, blazing bonfire. Over and over again. Right through the flames. Laughing and screaming and whooping it up. I have no memory of anyone getting hurt. Amazing. Friggin' amazing.

We all lived. We all survived. To this day, I still don't know how. I swear that during my teen years God Himself was guarding me.

As my teen years progressed so did my use. My drinking became worse. I'd done a sales job on myself and bought the lie that this drug-and-drinking hideout was the best. Friends, who were once wild with me, though, began backing away.

Tom was still loyal, but we were beginning to run in different groups. Tom was moving on. He got unscrewed up while I got deeper into heavier and stronger drugs. I'm not sure what happened to Lydia, but Tom got a job with a company that did drug screening, and somewhere along the way, he discovered health. After numerous attempts at various junior colleges, I went to work for my parents, which was a very good job for my addictions. It kept them hidden and safe.

I developed an organized routine: I would use meth-amphetamines during the day, alcohol at night, and then Seconal on Sundays, and I'd still show up for work every day as scheduled. Hallucinogens were a treat I used whenever I could find them.

I had a new cast of supporting characters. I found a bunch of new friends who, I was astounded to discover, could drink as much as or more than I did. And the suppliers I bought drugs from were all using. I could justify what I was doing as I looked out at those around me.

Excuses and justification are alive and well in the land of *no*. There was always a good reason to use, and I always knew someone who was using or abusing more than I was, so how messed up could I have been? This rationalization held true for me whether I was referring to those who could not see what I was doing or to those who were right in the pit with me. I had traded in the tree house for drugs, cocktails, and booze. I may not have been able to smell pine, but I was hidden and felt safe.

Le Turd

From 1968 until November 1984, I systematically put my body in harm's way. I abandoned my intellect and buried my emotions. I did it with drugs and Southern Comfort. Others do it with eighty-hour workweeks, super-sized meals, and diets of blame, complaints, and despair.

Everyone has their own way of dealing with shame. It's often a matter of convenience. It was for me. By late 1983 and early 1984, it had become increasingly difficult to hide my drinking. I had been told I had a drinking problem, and I should cut back. Oh, really? No problem, I just upped my consumption of cocaine. It was not difficult because I was seeing a psychiatrist who prescribed drugs that, in theory, would take away my alcohol cravings. Drugs, prescribed by a doctor, that I could use for a good reason! I liked that psychiatrist!

He came in handy when Michelle and I had a trip planned to go to Zihuatanejo and Puerto Vallarta, and I did not want to get into any more trouble in Mexico. I asked the good doctor to prescribe something so I wouldn't use. I took those pills faithfully. And then we met a couple on the end of their honeymoon.

They were gracious enough to share their last quarter ounce of cocaine. The three of us did some tasty shots of Tequila mixed in with plenty of poolside margaritas. It was a time to celebrate their marriage and wonderful future together, so I ordered bottle after bottle of Dom Pérignon, which we then proceeded to spit—yes, spit—at each other. I was in Mexico, taking an anti-craving medication, snorting up coke, swigging back Tequila and margaritas, and spitting twenty-year-old champagne at strangers. And I thought this was *fun*. Michelle never joined me in any of this fun. She was growing tired of my idea of fun.

It was during this time in Zihuatanejo that I met a man who was a kicker. I thought he was on a soccer team or football team. However he didn't appear athletic. He looked strong, but not athletic. I asked what team he played for. He explained that his team made it possible for me to get my supply. His job on the team was to kick bales of cannabis out of the planes that landed in Florida. The planes would load up in Mexico and land in Florida. The kicker kicked out the product that I wanted. How coincidental that we would actually meet, the kicker and the user. In 1982, he had made $100,000 playing kicker for his team. That is *all* he did, kick pot. I have never thought of a kicker in the same way since. Talking with him, the thought occurred to me that many little boys have dreams of becoming professional athletes, maybe a quarterback or a pitcher, and this man was once a small boy. Was his dream to someday become a world class soccer kicker? Would his kick on the soccer field bring home the gold? Did he dream that dream? And had his *Yes* gotten kicked out of him?

As I went from overindulging episode to episode, Michelle was with me through them all. She was there the night of our friend's thirtieth birthday party, as I did shot after shot, took over the P.A. system, got in a fight, and threw up. Never one to stay down, I drank some more and joined a mariachi band that was there to entertain. It may have been a good decision had I been a mariachi musician. I wasn't. But the fact that I was not had no bearing on my decision to march and sing and try to borrow some poor guy's instruments. Facts had nothing to do with me wowing my audience, or so I thought, with songs of love and hate that I sang in my idea of Spanish. Facts had nothing to do with my belief that I was entertaining and everybody sure loved me. My disregard of facts had Michelle on the phone a good portion of the next day apologizing to all of the people who had a different version of my facts.

Back at work, I knew so many people who seemed to love my version of things. We were involved a great deal with the media. The media people loved me. When I drank, I entertained, told jokes, and engaged in bizarre behavior. The media folk who sold us advertising loved what I did, usually.

One evening when we took a business cruise with this group, we were on shore in some brightly colored port, all doing shots of Clear Light. This is basically raw alcohol. Coincidently, we were again in Mexico. The taxi drivers there drove VW Bugs. Out of the blue, as we were riding in our cab, I decided I would entertain a lively group of touristas by standing on the top of our driver's Bug and making a spectacle of my hilarious self. I stood on the top of the moving taxi, shouted out jokes, and dove into the back seat, laughing uproariously at the hit I had been. The driver showed his appreciation of my show by pressing his revolver squarely into my cheek. I don't understand Spanish unless I am singing drunken, made-up mariachi tunes, but my guess is that he told me to never do that again. The rest of the trip back to the ship was less than festive.

I believed that this, of course, was just another great story people would later tell their friends back home, and it really was a good thing that had happened. Again, my version of the facts. It would be a great memory. A highlight, even. With that rationalization in mind, neither the somber mood in the cab, the gun in my face, nor the Spanish warning deterred me in the least. Perhaps the taxi ride was somber, perhaps Mexico just did not agree with me, but there was always the ship.

Each passenger on a ship is issued a whistle in case there is an emergency at sea. I took it upon myself to initiate another highlight for any passenger in the proximity of our cabin. I marched up and down the corridors blowing my whistle at four in the morning. The next day the cruise director made a special stop at my cabin. I found out it is possible to have a helicopter land on the ship and escort out-of-control travelers off the ship. My adventures on that trip earned me an invitation to Le Turd. Le Turd is a club whose logo is a pile of dog crap. Its ranks included drunks, deviates, and rejects from the media industry. I was invited to join their elite group. All my desperate attempts to numb the shame of being me and drown the fear that I was worthless led me to that moment of certainty. I was now an official pile of shit.

Joining that club was a turning point for me. It triggered something that produced a picture I could see in front of me: huge, ominous clouds, full of rain and thunder, dismal and dark, a category five catastrophe, loomed, heading straight for me. The shame of Le Turd didn't stop me from the binge drinking weekend in New York, and probably triggered it. But it was there with me as I sat on that window ledge. *Jump, turd!*

Soul-Shrinking

Addiction is an illness, like diabetes or heart disease. An addiction such as alcoholism progresses with specific symptoms and degenerative results, just like any other chronic disease that is left untreated. I learned all that when I was in rehab. After much observation, education, and reflection, I realized that the difference between heart disease, diabetes, and alcoholism is that the alcohol not only eats away at your body, it eats away at your soul.

Diabetes may be a disease of the pancreas, but addiction is the disease of the spirit. Just as you can prevent, manage, and lessen the damage of diabetes, you can prevent, manage, and lessen the damage of alcoholism, drug addiction, and the myriad of other addictions that run rampant in our country.

When our shame tells us *no,* when it declares that we have no potential, the process of *soul-shrinking* begins. By 1973, I was twenty-one, and actively involved in the shrinking of my soul. I had told myself I was a popular rebel, but the real me was hiding. My focus was *no,* and my belief was *no.*

My life has been and continues to be lived in extremes. Nothing I do today or have done in the past is ever middle-of-the-road. I may not be the norm, yet I believe that like me, most people give up the *Yes* in their hearts soon after they are born. If you don't believe me, get out some old photos of yourself as a child. When did the look in your eyes change? You know the look I'm talking about. The free, unhidden, happy, look-at-me, ain't-I-great, big eyed, vulnerable, look-right-into-the-camera-lens look that most little kids have. It morphs from that into a guarded, half-real smile. And as such, it conveys not unbridled joy, but only a measured cooperation, like, "I'm smiling because you asked, but I'm not really happy." When did your look change?

Mine changed when I realized that who I was and what I was was wrong, yet I had no idea how to change it. My spark in the early photos, standing with my brother and sisters, either left or was buried somewhere before I was eight years old. I had stopped believing in me. A belief and trust in oneself is a major part of the true definition of what it is to live a *Yes*-centered life. Conversely, when we believe that we are incapable or do not matter, when we believe there are no answers or that we are at the mercy of the world, we live a *no*-centered life.

My lack of belief in the world and in myself shaped much of what I did and how I behaved. My shame told me I had no value, and, as I accepted that belief, I acted in alignment with it. People who value themselves take care of their bodies, their minds, and their emotions. Living deep in my *no*, I just couldn't get there.

The Light of *Yes*

The first time I boarded a commercial airliner on a cloudy day, I was amazed to notice that as we gained altitude the haze and fog disappeared and the sun shone brightly. Even during my lost days of long blackouts, the sweaty nights of desperate scrambling to find the last molecule of coke, and the fuzzy sunrises of marijuana-induced philosophizing, *Yes* shone somewhere, a light above the murk, waiting for me to wake up, rise, and allow it to live within me again.

In November 1984, I saw it only as a distant speck of light shining through the black storm clouds. By some grace or miracle to which I remain hugely indebted, I decided to focus on that light. I decided to do whatever it took to keep *Yes* alive.

The first *Yes* I allowed to enter my life and decided to cherish and care for like it was my child was sobriety. I decided that it could be possible, that it was possible, and that I would find the way to make sobriety possible for me. I had found my *Yes*. I was on my way.

Yes is not a clever sales technique or a sneaky way to have more sex, though staying in a place of *Yes* opened doors I did not even realize had been closed. What *Yes* is, and what it became inside me, is a certainty, a belief. When I got to my place of *Yes*, I finally could believe in the possibility and the potential that was me.

Twelve-Step and self-support groups teach that you must want sobriety to attain it. They teach that if one person can attain it, anyone is able to attain it. The belief of thousands who came before me became my belief. Of course, when I was living in the belief that nothing was possible, that good was something someone else got, I was also following a belief held by thousands, even millions of people who came before me.

What had changed was my decision. I made a very conscious decision to focus on light. I control my own *Yes*. It's really that simple. That decision made me view the entire world from a different perspective. If I could make a decision that changed what I believed and how I felt, anything was possible. I knew it. I believed it. I felt it. I had now turned on the light of *Yes* that had been shut off when *I* decided to shut it off. Now I had my *Yes*. I had no idea of where that one *Yes* would take me, but I knew it wouldn't be a comfort zone or a hiding place.

Freeing the Soul

In the early days of my recovery, I was given the assignment of finding Scotty and his tree house. My job was to get Scotty out of the tree and let him know that he didn't have to hide any more, that it was okay and just as safe to be the hero he dreamed of being. I had scoffed a bit at all that Inner Child psychology. Since we're supposed to be focusing on becoming responsible adults, some addicts balk at this kind of delving into the past. There was a lot we were being asked to look at.

Sometimes it took all my courage and willingness to face it. I was willing to leave the comforting ego-prop of pretending I was too adult to revisit my childhood self because I believed my rehab team when they reassured me that this step would help me get sober.

The way back is sometimes more painful than being there. Driving through my old neighborhood, I heard all the names the kids called me. I felt the painful frustration, ridicule, intimidation, and shame. When I got to the spot, I stopped the car and peered out at an eerie sight. The tree was gone. The tree house was nowhere to be seen, as if it had never existed. I was immediately flushed with all sorts of feelings: sadness that my fortress had been demolished, confusion that I had never once considered that it might be gone, and then a gentle relief that I could finally bring closure to that world of the misfit who had to hide to feel safe. At last I understood that hiding places and comfort zones deny a belief in one's true spirit and are part of *no*.

I got out and walked around. Some of the avocado trees were still there. The house looked smaller, but the scene was essentially familiar. The kids peddling their bikes around me and the unmistakable smells of the old neighborhood had me traveling backward in time, and I saw it all. I could see the tree, real as could be, the tree house, and the rope ladder. And I saw Scotty climbing down that rope, out of that tree, his shoulders slumped and his head down, like he was headed somewhere he really didn't want to go. He was kicking at a stone as he scuffled slowly, and then a piece of old tin. I saw him take a breath, square his skinny shoulders, and stick his chin out with resolve. I watched him straighten up and look at the back door of the house, determined to face whatever awaited him that day.

He was there. I hadn't lost him. And he was tougher than I remembered. The tree had been cut down, but not him. He's still there, and now he's winning.

Courage and Willingness to Leave the Comfort Zone/ Hiding Place involves:
- Understanding the pull of *no* in your life in dealing with fear and shame
- Understanding that addictions are soul-shrinking
- Understanding that there will always be excuses and rationalizations to follow your addiction
- Understanding that addictions are comfort zones and hiding places
- Understanding that living in your comfort zone/ hiding place is a denial of your *Yes*
- Understanding that living in your comfort zone/ hiding place has consequences
- Becoming willing to come out of hiding and explore the healing potential outside the comfort zone
- Opening yourself to the courage to follow your *Yes*.

If you feel as if there is a ball and chain around your life, it may be because that is your comfort zone. Letting go of comfort zones is a profound process with implications for everyone, not just addicts.

CHAPTER 6

Get Out Your Comfort Zone

Saying *Yes* to the Universe is not for people who crave comfort. Far from bringing comfort, following a higher vision and listening to the *Yes* that is deep within brings great discomfort and sometimes pain. Heroes do not necessarily have more courage or a more daring spirit than the average person. What they have is the willingness to act and to face discomfort.

Staying in a comfort zone is hardly a guarantee of comfort. But stretching beyond it is a guarantee that you will grow.

What about going to work? A recent Gallup poll found that about seventy-seven percent of Americans hate their jobs. In a report by CareerBuilder.com, *Retail Workers 2005*, forty-eight percent of the retail workers surveyed said that they do not look forward to going to work each day. If seven out of ten are in jobs they don't like, I have to ask these questions: Why is that acceptable to them? Why do so many individuals stay in a place of *no* day in and day out? Millions of people do this, daily! When I gather with ten of my friends, seven of them dislike getting up in the morning. I can hear the excuses: bills have to be paid, food has to be bought, and, my favorite, "No one likes their job."

What if these seven people could find some positives in

their job? Perhaps the *Yes* could be the people they work with or gratitude for a regular paycheck. What if they could get out of bed in the morning feeling passionate, interested, and excited? Would they be healthier or their futures brighter? How would it benefit the people they live with? How would it benefit me and the world I live in if the people around me just got a little bit happier? If they felt a bit more relevant.

We all have a number of directions in which we can look to find inspiration, motivation, *Yes*. Some people just don't know how to look, or where to look. Some are looking, but they are looking in the wrong places, places they will never find *Yes*. Gangs can seem attractive, offering acceptance and a sense of belonging, but they are no place to find *Yes*. Where is the family to offer them this sense of belonging? Drugs offer escape, instant results, and a false sense of security. But drugs lead their victims further away from *Yes*, and deeper toward *no*. When will we no longer tolerate a world in which drugs take some our brightest lights away? Crime can seem to solve a person's urgent problems, but it creates bigger, long-term ones. This is not a place to make excuses or assign blame. However, we need to wake up and realize that when one of us is not living a life of *Yes*, the life we're designed to live, all of us are affected.

I watch people who are in emotional pain daily. They may have a druggie daughter or son. Perhaps they have told themselves there is nowhere to go in their job or career. Some are in damaging relationships. They all appear to have one thing in common: they are afraid of leaving what they know because they fear the possible pain of the unknown. They continue to do what they have always done and think they are staying comfortable. So, they continue to get the same results and then complain about what is happening in their life.

How crazy is it that people who are not willing to *be*

uncomfortable, are willing to *stay* uncomfortable. I now tell my clients, "Find a strong reason to change and then be ready to work through some pain." I also say, "If it's tough, do it. If it's easy, you are not changing."

Pinball Change

Deciding to live a *Yes*-centered life requires you to be willing enough and courageous enough for focused change. A lot of people believe they are growing whenever they change part of their lives. They change jobs, they change hair color, they change wives or husbands, they change where they live. They change things in their outer life and say, "I change all the time." I call this Pinball Change. In Pinball Change, there is a lot of bumping and redirecting and then more bumping and redirecting. Eventually you are bumped off the playing field. Those practicing Pinball Change are bumping and moving and have no idea why. Maybe it's for the sake of moving. Maybe they feel they can fool themselves and the world by saying, "Look at how I am working so hard, trying new things. See how I'm trying!"

It's like someone who reads every book they can find about swimming—the joys of swimming, how to swim, how to swim better, how to swim different strokes, how to swim in different conditions, and on and on. And then they never get in the water! Who are they kidding?

They change jobs, change partners, change locations. They keep moving with absolutely no idea of where they are moving. Why not get in a car, turn on the ignition, and just start driving? No map, no directions, no clue. But, hey, they are driving! Without a clear *Yes* to be led by, it is almost impossible to go anywhere worth going. They will arrive somewhere, sure, but they will have no reason to be there. Then, they'll take off and repeat the same pointless process again and again.

GPS Change

As human beings, we are always changing. Our bodies change, the world we live in changes, family members die or are born, our lives are different. Our lives change, and yet our attitudes, our beliefs, and our behaviors don't always change as we go along. They stagnate. It is amazing to see what happens when you focus on changing a specific something and you clearly know why you are doing it. It becomes easier, like driving with a GPS.

When people know what they want and why they want it, others show up to help. There is less stumbling and more succeeding. Your steps take you forward, not in circles. You end the day with a feeling of success and accomplishment. Basically, you just feel better!

My Life as a Pinball

In 1976, I was twenty-two years old. My drinking and partying remained, for the most part, a weekend and nighttime experience, but it was enough to worry my parents. I was working on and off in their shops, dating here and there, having a brief go at candle-making and generally drifting downward. My mother said, "Why don't you travel? Go someplace, find yourself." A few other people gave me the same advice, so I decided that is what I would do.

I didn't waste any time. It wasn't long before I had a passport, great new hiking boots, a beautiful new backpack, and a rugged-looking new windbreaker to handle any nasty weather. I decided I was going to backpack through Europe. I was Jewish, and most Jewish individuals are not campers. Hiking, backpacking, windbreakers, camping—they were all words that I had heard, and they sounded good. Of course, I had never done any of this before and had no idea what I was getting myself into. Still, not being familiar with something had never stopped me in the past and would not stop me in the future. I wanted to backpack through Europe for a year. I did not think ahead about how I would afford it, what I would do, or where I would stay. I just thought of what I wanted and jumped in with both feet and all my new stuff.

I left California bound for Israel. My mother had some distant relatives there, so it seemed to me a logical place to start. I did have a vague dream that on the other side of the ocean I might discover a purpose that would make me want to dry out and get my head on straight. The beautiful new backpack was stuffed as tightly as I could stuff it. I tied the great new boots to the outside of it. I felt good in the new, rugged-looking windbreaker I had purchased for my adventure. When I got to the San Diego airport, the beautiful new backpack came in overweight, so I stuffed the pockets of my rugged-looking windbreaker with the heaviest objects I had packed. It was stuffed and stretched down to my knees. So much for that outdoor, rugged look that I was going for, but they let me on the plane. It was a sacrifice I was willing to make.

The plane stopped in New York, where I had to catch my connection on El Al Airlines. I had never been to an airport on my own. No one told me there were different terminals, domestic and international. How ridiculous! Someone motioned to a place outside to get a shuttle and told me I had to take to get to this ridiculous International Terminal. I went outside in my stretched-out windbreaker. I found wind chill and I found ice, but I found no shuttle. I walked over a mile to get to what I now referred to as The Effing Ridiculous International Terminal.

I left Southern California without giving any thought to what New York weather might be like. The sun was out in California, but the sun was not out in New York. It was snowing and probably something like 30 degrees below zero. It felt like that, anyway. The windbreaker had been a good idea in California. The once rugged-looking windbreaker, now thoroughly wet and stretched down to my knees, was a bad idea for the New York cold and snow. How could people live in weather like this? I couldn't wait to leave. But first I had to catch my international flight at The Effing Ridiculous International Terminal.

I was extremely freezing and extremely mad by the time I reached The Effing Ridiculous International Terminal. But once I got there, no one cared about how cold I was or how I felt. They didn't give a rat's ass about me. Still, there must have been something that endeared me to the El Al agents, because they pulled me off to the side and frisked me, freezing, in my new windbreaker.

This was before the security procedures we now have to pass through at all U.S. airports. But not if you were boarding an El Al flight. If you were flying to Israel on an Israeli airline, you went through a security procedure. In July 1976, an Air France airliner had been hijacked by Palestinian and German terrorists and flown to Uganda. I had no desire to go to Uganda, or to be hijacked anywhere for that matter, so I was in complete agreement that El Al take all the precautions it felt was warranted. I was on my way to Europe, and I wanted to get there!

I got to Israel and found my mother's distant relatives. I had begun my adventure. In 1976, if you were Jewish, in Israel, and under the age of twenty-five, you were expected to volunteer on a kibbutz. What is a kibbutz? It was where I wanted to go.

Two days later, I was on a cot, my gear stashed, waiting to find out how I could help build a better Israel. At 2:00 in the morning, I found out. "Wake up, Scott, we have your assignment." It was dark as I got on a truck that took me to a very long, low building. I imagine it was about the size of five buildings. I was dropped off at one end and told to go inside. I still had no idea of what I was to do, but I could hear lots of what sounded like shrieking, and I could smell the unmistakable smell of shit.

My imagination began to take over as the shrieking and smells continued unabated.

Finally, some person in charge handed me gloves and showed me the chickens. Hundreds and hundreds and hundreds of chickens. Not shrieking, but squawking. Squawking at the top of their little chicken lungs. Squawking and terrified. Running around like, well, terrified, squawking chickens. My job was to catch the terrified, squawking chickens and throw them in crates, seal the crates, and stack the crates.

Have you ever tried to catch terrified, squawking chickens? It's not easy. You grab them by the legs, once you finally catch one. Those buggers can run fast on their terrified little chicken feet. You grab one and toss it into a crate. Then, as fast as you can, you put the top on the crate and go chase another chicken.

Do you have any idea what chickens do when you grab them by the legs and toss them into a crate? They pee and poop. Everywhere. In all directions. It makes sense, if you think about it. They're terrified, and they're being grabbed and tossed. I had on gloves and my great new hiking/chicken-grabbing boots and no other protective gear, which would have come in handy to protect me from the pee and poop.

The real problem came when I started stacking the chicken crates. They stacked about six or seven high. I am not all that tall, certainly not nearly tall enough to be above the terrified, peeing and pooping chickens. What a way to break in my great new hiking boots!

9:00 a.m. finally came, and back I went to my cot and a shower. In 1976, an Israel kibbutz shower meant nothing but cold water. I was freezing again. I was so ready for comfort but not ready to give up volunteering for Israel.

I graduated from chicken-crater to irrigation system installer. I actually enjoyed this until the Kibbutz found out I was a

California boy and decided I needed a different job. I was then taken to the other side of the chicken building where chicken poop needed to be shoveled to a place where it could actually be used. I was certain this was helping Israel, but I was uncertain in what exact way.

The shoveling made my back hurt. Well, that is what I told my supervisor when I asked for another assignment. "Hey, Scott, you can leave whenever you want" was the supervisor's response. I heard that as "take it or leave it," so I left it. Gladly. I left, but I had learned there was a limit to being unfocused, under committed, and uncomfortable. At least I found my limit.

The time that I spent in the kibbutz I spent totally sober. I did not drink, and there were absolutely no drugs, not even marijuana. I started out being willing: willing to try on sobriety, willing to do what the leaders asked of me, willing to have a positive attitude. But I gave up when the work and living environment became more uncomfortable than I had bargained for. I did not allow myself to change during my time in Israel. I *said* I was willing, but I was lying. I absolutely did not allow myself to change, I allowed myself to adapt—a pinball change. Had I experienced a GPS change, I would not have gone on to Greece where I met the girls who took me to Turkey.

When I got to Turkey, I discovered that my money had been stolen in Greece. I arrived at the hostel where I was staying in Turkey and gave the man my passport and camera as collateral while I went to the U.S. Embassy to contact the bank to wire more money. I didn't have a charge card, but I did have an arrangement with my bank at home to wire money to me from my very small account as I traveled in Europe. Back then, it took about three or four days to wire money. So, there I was in Turkey with no contacts, no money, and no way to get around except by bus.

I still had my California driver's license. I would get on a

Turkish bus, flash my California license, sternly mutter "Interpol" and move towards the back of the bus. The drivers never questioned me. I was twenty-two, American, and had a very good-looking, somewhat stretched-out windbreaker and hiking boots that reeked of chicken pee and poop. Somehow they either accepted I was from Interpol or feared I was a nut case and did not want to make trouble.

Whatever, it worked. I would go from my cold-water youth hostel to the other side of the city and hang out at a Hyatt or a Hilton. Despite my childhood loner days of social rejection, people liked me, and the charm I'd learned in my early drug-using phase still worked. I had no problems. I would strike up a conversation with well-to-do Americans who were staying at the hotel, and they would usually end up inviting me to lunch or breakfast. I ate well, and then used the luxurious men's room to wash and clean up with honest-to-goodness hot water. I was blessed!

I never thought that I could not make any of this happen, and I was willing to do whatever it took to survive until the money came from my bank.

I did not contact my parents, but the bank did. Even though I had made the bank promise not to inform my mother or father, someone at the bank thought that a twenty-two-year-old kid, alone in Turkey with no money, needed to have his family alerted. I got a message at my hostel from the embassy that I needed to call home. Thoughts of illness or an accident back in California went through my head as I traveled on one bus and then another to get to the embassy where I could place the call. I was worried and also a little scared.

My parents, on the other side of the ocean, were also feeling worried and scared. They had spent twenty-two years witnessing my chaos-creating ability. Now they were being told by the bank that they should call me. I don't know what thoughts went through their minds, but I have a pretty good idea.

I have never been good with numbers, and I badly miscalculated the difference in time zones between Turkey and California. The phone next to my mother and father's bed rang at 2:00 a.m. I'm sure they feared the worst as they said hello, only to find out I was fine. By the time I called, my money had come through, I told them, and I was staying in Turkey. I went back to the hostel, and my mother and father went back to sleep.

Drug raids were common in Turkey during the late 1970s. I was told that Turkey and the U.S. had a wacky agreement whereby the U.S. would pay Turkey $11 a day for each American Turkey picked up for drug trafficking and kept in jail. Thank you very much, U.S. government!

That didn't stop me. I got high daily. I was a ripe candidate for plucking, but I never kept drugs on me, and I never hid a stash for anyone to find. Whenever I wanted to get some, I knew people who knew people, and it was always easy to meet people who had things to sell. You could just walk into a local bar or meet young people through the various hostels who had hash or marijuana available.

I would not hold on to any drug no matter how potent. Never. No way. I may have been doing stupid things, but even I knew that would be a stupid chance to take. I only needed to dream about Turkish prisons, what they must be like, and what they did to Americans in exchange for that $11 bounty.

I stayed at a hostel in Turkey with young people from all over the globe. I roomed with a male prostitute from Switzerland, a German who was a real, live gangster, and a Malaysian kid who'd had no bellybutton since the time someone stabbed him. I soon understood why someone might stab him.

Almost every day, I'd smoke hash and read. They went together. For some reason, hash made me want to read. So one day, I was relaxing, reading, enjoying my day, and the Raid of the Turkish Gestapo began. Into the hostel they came, patted me down, checked my pack and left. In and out, before I could run, or say *hi* in Turkish, or plead innocent.

Moments later, Mr. No Belly Button entered the room. "What were they here for?" he wanted to know.

"The regular drill, you know, check my pockets, ask about drugs, try and get their $11-a-day American."

The Malaysian turned white and told me to get off my bunk.

"What?" I didn't get it.

"Just get off your bunk." He said it again with a little more force.

I was in a pretty mellow mood and did what he said. He then retrieved *his* stash from *my* bunk! Mellow left abruptly and serious anger showed up. In fact, the anger went from, "He did what?" to "I am going to kill him!" in about two seconds. I beat the crap out of him and then crammed my beautiful, but by now battered backpack with my possessions and said *Gülegüle* to Turkey.

My time in Turkey was a duplication of my time in the States. I partied, I took risks with my health, and I hid what I was doing for fear of arrest. When I left Turkey, I was back to drinking and doping, reacting without thinking or feeling. My brief stint at sobriety was over, and I was heading deeper into addiction.

After Turkey, I went to Rome and then to Amsterdam. While in Turkey I had been able to purchase an International Student Pass through the black market. With this pass I was able to get dirt-cheap flights. Rome was not for me. I did the tourist thing, saw the Coliseum, and ate some pasta, but after Turkey, it all seemed too normal, too commonplace, a little boring. The excitement, the living from moment to moment that I experienced in Turkey was not happening in Rome. It was 1976, and I had heard about Amsterdam. Away I flew.

To get the feel of a city, go to the center of the town and sit. You'll see who is doing what, the expressions on people's faces, and the caution level of the city. I sat in the middle of Amsterdam, in Dam Square, feeling the sun on my back, smoking a cigarette, and enjoying the day and the feel of being out of the confines of Rome. I was enjoying the scenery and allowing the energy of this beautiful city to seep into my awareness. I took in a deep breath and smelled pot. All my senses revved up. I looked around and saw a kid a little younger than me walking and smoking a "J" in the center of the frigging city!

I wanted to believe that what I was seeing was legal. I really wanted to believe. I had been in Turkey living in its militia attitude towards drugs, so I tensed automatically. I had smoked hash and marijuana while I was in the land of zero tolerance, but I always did it looking over my shoulder and taking great care that no one would find out and arrest me. I had even done that in the States. Now I was in the middle of a large European city, and here was some stranger walking around smoking dope. No one looked twice. This was remarkable! I looked around more carefully, and there were people everywhere with pipes—and it wasn't Sir Walter Raleigh they were smoking!

The kid sitting near me must have seen my amazement, and I asked him, "What gives?"

"Hey, it's legal. Haven't you heard? You're in Amsterdam. Come on, I'll show you."

I was a willing follower as he led me towards a local bar.

If you are a wine connoisseur you go to Napa or Sonoma, or maybe you go to France. You go and sample the top wines, you sample a large variety, and maybe you buy some. If you were a drug connoisseur in 1976, you went to an Amsterdam bar. It was legit, and I got to sample. Black Afghani, Thai Sticks, Colombian Red. There was Gold Bond from Lebanon and hash, hash, hash! It was all available and all cheap. In the U.S. hash was going for

$25 to $30 a gram (if you could even get it), and in Amsterdam in 1976 I could buy it for $3 to $4 a gram. Unbelievable.

I have always been an entrepreneur. I cashed in what was left of my traveler's checks and bought as much hash as I could afford. I could sell, and I could sell legally. The hotel I was staying at was run by an Israeli with whom I hit it off. He told me that he would pay me about a guilder (the equivalent of about 50 cents in 1976) for every person who I brought to the hotel. I would hang out at the train station and profile the travelers departing the trains. It was easy to tell who was from California: they'd have on flip flops and T-shirts. We had something in common, California.

"Looking for a good hotel?" I'd say. I'd take them to the hotel, collect my guilders, and then sell them hash for about $15 a gram and collect more money. They would normally share what they just bought with me, their new friend. We were all happy. Everyone won. The thought of staying right in Amsterdam was very tempting, but my partying eventually sent me home.

While I was in Amsterdam my drinking escalated as I smoked some great hash. It was one huge party for Scott H. Silverman. During one of my drinking sprees, I staggered into the men's room and noticed a chunk of glass on the floor. My warped-on-Thai-stick-and-booze brain thought it would be a great idea to try and step on the glass. To this day, I still don't know what I was trying to accomplish—crush the glass, show off to my buddies, or just kill myself. What I do know is that some time after I stepped on the glass. I noticed my shoe was filled with what felt like water. It turned out not to be water, but blood.

Two days later, the pain in my foot was intense. The thought of medical help crossed my mind, but my money philosophy was get it, spend it, get it, spend it. I had no reserve cash, certainly not enough to go to a doctor. So, I waited, thinking my throbbing foot would just get better. This philosophy can bring on a load of grief. Pain is a clue that we must take more aggressive action than ignoring it.

The disease of addiction is loaded with the belief that "it" will all magically just get better. Something or someone will come and rescue the situation, and the pain will disappear. This kind of thinking persists because change always occurs. We are growing, or we are shrinking. When we seem to be stagnating, we are merely being forced to change by toxicity. Stagnate long enough and, just like a stagnant body of water, you become toxic. My wait-and-see philosophy about my foot brought toxicity. By the fourth day my foot was on fire. The pain I felt drove me to seek help.

Then I learned that Amsterdam had socialized medicine. The doctor was amazed I had been living with all the pain caused by the glass buried in the flesh of my foot. I did not tell him that I had hoped drugging and drinking would kill the pain while everything got better. This idea that somehow the pain of my life would get magically better as I drank and drugged was a microcosm of every area of my life. It *was* my life.

The doctor removed the glass and sutured my foot. Meanwhile, my inebriated brain began to realize that I might just hurt myself in bigger and more serious ways if I stayed in Amsterdam. I had a small awakening. The history of my substance abuse, if graphed, would show these small awakenings. I would party, party, party, get in trouble or get hurt, and then I'd cut back for a bit, only to go forward with renewed zeal once the emergency was past. This is symptomatic of the disease of addiction.

I still had about three months left of my stay in Europe, but I decided to go home. The foot incident had scared me. I came home an accomplished hustler, even deeper into the drug and alcohol scene. I took my place in the family business, where, over the next three years, I drank and drugged to such blackout stage that much of what I did can only be told by others. I don't remember what I did between the time I was twenty-two and twenty-five. What I do know is that somehow, through some type of miracle, I survived.

Sure, I had good intentions from time to time. But good intentions alone are inadequate as a motivation. They lead to superficial changes that can leave you in worse shape than you were before. But, hey, I tried, right?

On my journey, I had no commitment to change, and I didn't ask for help. My *Yes* was nowhere in sight. I retreated into my comfort zone, still hiding from the real me. I used all kinds of rationalizations—it's legal here—to stay in hiding. I lacked the willingness and courage to get out of the comfort zone. I made a *pinball* change, careening around, reacting, arriving at a point directly opposite my original intentions instead of making the true *GPS* change that would have prevented the damage that led to my window-ledge moment.

Bottoming Out

Waiting for a dire crisis before taking action is typical of addicts and, in fact, symptomatic of our world today. We seem to take action only when emergencies occur, yet the change and the action need to happen *before* the catastrophe. We need to take action while we *still feel comfortable* instead of waiting for the pain to show up and force us to act.

I waited until I was in a hole, a very deep hole, before I started the long climb up and out. My hope is that others will not need to get to a place where they are backed into a corner with only the two alternatives of death and change. Yes, that way, the way I did it, does work. It is called bottoming out. But the destruction caused by getting to the bottom can be avoided. People need to be willing to be uncomfortable *now* and embrace the goal of moving forward through the discomfort and into a place of inner responsibility and power. There may not be a shortcut to *Yes,* but *Yes* can be a shortcut to preventing bottoming out.

Some people are so afraid of losing, they wait until there is nothing to lose. To them I would say, "There are winners, and there are learners!"

- Unhappy people have one thing in common: they are afraid of leaving a comfort zone
- Any change less than a committed willingness to leave the comfort zone will simply move you around like a ball in a machine
- Embracing a *Yes*-centered life requires willingness and courage for focused change, a *GPS* change.
- A GPS change is real, tangible change and it can prevent bottoming out

CHAPTER 7

Willingness
and Courage

I always had a list of what I wanted in a wife. My list was similar to the list of what my mother wanted for me, but I never let my mother know that. It was my secret until I knew Michelle was the woman I wanted to marry.

Michelle was my younger sister's friend, and I thought of her as a kid, one of the girls who were in and out of our house. I called her "the brat." I had known her and her family for a long time, but it took an illness for me to see what had always been there.

Until I actually noticed Stacy's beautiful friend, I was having a running dialogue with my mother concerning who I was going to marry. I would tell her that I was thinking of marrying Mary Katherine, a Catholic, or Midge, an older woman with two small children. My mother was and is committed to Judaism and wanted her children to marry inside the faith and give her Jewish grandchildren. She is a very wise woman who has always believed that marriage is tough enough when your backgrounds are similar. My mother, a woman of commitment, desired that when and if I committed to a woman, that woman would be able to commit to Judaism, to grandchildren, and to me. She did not meet my choices in love, or at least what I told her were my choices, with smiles and good luck wishes. Quite the opposite.

Our conversations fed my rebellious spirit while they caused my mother sleepless nights. They also gave me a small inner laugh.

Then Michelle became sick—severely sick. She was hospitalized with bacterial meningitis. "Michelle could be dying," my mother said. My sisters and brother weren't around, and most of Michelle's other friends were away at college. "You should call her," my mother told me. Sometimes my mother can be overly dramatic, but sometimes the drama is warranted. So I called Michelle that day…and the day after…and the day after that. I began to see Michelle, hoping she'd look past my addictions and see something worthwhile. She was twenty-one and had her own secret list of what she wanted in a husband. I don't believe that drug addict or alcoholic was on her list, but I must have had enough of the other traits she was looking for. For myself, I realized very early in our dating life that she had almost everything on my list.

We dated in secret. She was living in Los Angeles at the time, and I was living in San Diego. We would meet in Palm Springs or some other point in between. It became clear to both of us that we were involved in more than a passing infatuation. Neither of us wanted our families to be involved in what was ultimately our decision. It was very complicated. Michelle and Stacy were still best friends, and I knew that if my mother found out that I was dating a trusted, beautiful friend of the family, there would be no stopping her interference. There was also the question of what we'd do if it did not work out. Michelle did not want to lose a very good friend, and I did not want to be asked a myriad list of "what happened?" questions.

Michelle was concerned that her parents would object because of my bad reputation. She also knew that both of our parents would want to be involved in what were our hopes, our dreams. We knew the response we believed we would get from both sets of parents was normal; we just needed to explore the relationship before we involved them. Michelle finally initiated action based on her commitment. She knew I was basically lazy and would not be moving to L.A. She decided to move back to San Diego and into her parent's home. It would now be impossible to keep our deepening relationship to ourselves. After nine months of secrecy, I asked her parents for permission to marry her.

Michelle's mother had one question:"Is it true what we have heard about you, Scott?"

My response was, "No one will take better care of your daughter than I will." I meant it with every cell of my being. I loved this woman and wanted to spend the rest of my life with her.

I broke the news to my parents by asking my mother for my grandmother's ring. "Mom, remember when you told me that I could have Grandma's ring when the time came to marry? Well, I think I need that ring now." I am pretty sure my mother was worried that the treasured ring might be heading to an older woman or a person who would want to raise children in a different faith. She only asked one question, "Do I know her?" To say my answer brought happiness to Maggie Silverman is an understatement.

Michelle soon showed me how she defined commitment. Her commitment was to me and to our marriage. My commitment was to her, to working, and to partying. Eventually my commitments other than partying wavered, but Michelle remained steadfast. She grew tired, but she stayed with me. When she woke up at 4:00 a.m. in an empty bed, she would know that I was out finding sources of cocaine and she would go out and find me. I never resented her during this time. In fact I admired her and my respect for her grew.

When she said the words "in sickness and in health," she really meant them. When she said "for richer or poorer," she did not say "unless I change my mind." She was and continues to be my number one supporter, my best friend, and my sounding board, even when I took her patient and unconditional commitment to me for granted and indulged my addictions.

Everybody's Doing It

Marrying Michelle did not slow down my partying, but it changed how I did it. I became a binge drinker. I would hold off on the booze until I could hold off no longer, and then I would binge until I hit bottom, take a break, and then start again. When I wasn't drinking, I would use coke or marijuana. In 1979 and 1980, it was easy to convince myself that what I was doing was not that big of a problem because everybody was doing it. It was easy to kid myself. It was easy to tell Michelle that it was no big deal and everything would be okay. It was no big deal? It was no big deal until I slid from where I was to where I could no longer manage anything, not even my use. Then came New York, the ledge, and recovery. My love for Michelle hadn't stopped me from partying, but once I bottomed, I realized how much I cherished her gift of commitment. It helped me say, *do this for others* when I couldn't sober up for myself alone.

As I write this out, it sounds easy, even simple. Use drugs, get addicted, see no hope, hear *Yes*, get into recovery. Easy? It was not easy. It was a very big deal.

Willingness, Not Will Power

Recovery requires being willing to ask and receive help from others; it involves a fundamental surrender. Part of the surrender was already in place when I checked into rehab. I surrendered out on that ledge—yet there was another part of my will that was still kicking and screaming. This is that most difficult of all steps: stepping out of your Will and into Willingness.

I had to be willing to let others make decisions for me. This was almost impossible for me twenty-four years ago, and it remains an area I continue to struggle with daily.

Though rehab was the hardest thing I've ever done, by accepting the hands that were outstretched in my early days of recovery, I made it less difficult for me than I have heard others say it was for them. I was hearing my inner *Yes*, my family and Michelle were with me, I had the kites, and I was young. The toughest part of early recovery was what AA calls "surrender." It is one of the twelve steps a person has to take. The first three steps read:

1. We admitted we were powerless over alcohol— that our lives had become unmanageable.

2. We came to believe that a Power greater than ourselves could restore us to sanity.

3. We made a decision to turn our will and our lives over to the care of God *as we understood Him.*

The first was a cinch. No one needed to convince me that my life had become unmanageable or that I was powerless over my use of substances. I spent no time resisting this step. Steps two and three were tougher. It seemed as if I was being asked to give up...not just give up drugs and alcohol, but give up control. The word surrender was used often. It was not a word I liked then, and it is not a word I like now. I am a fighter; it is the premise behind *Tell Me No, I Dare You!* But my counselor, my sponsor, and my community were all asking me to surrender. It seemed to go against all that I believed in and all that I felt. It went against what I had learned in school, which was that surrender was not an option in war. To surrender meant you were weak and a coward. It was not an attractive thought. But I had to find a way to do it.

Surrender

I was being asked to be a passenger in my life, or that is what surrender seemed to mean. "Let go and let God." Great words, but I didn't know what they meant. Was I supposed to sit in the house or hang onto my kite strings, and my life would somehow get better? I wanted to know what I was supposed to *do*, not what I was supposed to surrender. It made sense to let go of drugs and alcohol. It made sense to let go of or surrender cravings. The question for me was how was I supposed to surrender the outcomes when dealing with people? This was all new, and it was all tough. It was very hard.

I finally decided that if I couldn't really surrender, I would decide to be *willing* to surrender. I made the decision to start with willingness. This one decision served me again and again. I still use this technique when I find I am struggling to control the uncontrollable. I decide to be willing to *surrender the outcome*. After I do this, a strange phenomenon happens: I get a physical feeling of release. It actually feels as if I am being released from bondage—my arms, my chest, all of me feels stronger! It's a paradox: surrender your power and feel more powerful.

Interdependence

Our country stresses individuality and self-reliance almost to a fault. I believe in individuality, and I teach self-reliance, but when someone clings to an *I-can-do-it-alone-I-need-no-one* attitude, it hurts all of us. It is the opposite of saying "I am helpless, someone must rescue me." Of course, this hurts the community as well. Often, neither overly dependent nor overly independent individuals can find their own *Yes*. What we need more of is *interdependence*.

In a world of interdependence, cooperation becomes

essential, and creative solutions are found. I look at the world, and I see how trees are dependent on the earth and the earth is dependent on the air and the air dependent on the trees. I believe that our world was created to be interdependent. It is a part of my *Yes* to acknowledge that I need people and that people need me. Interdependence works when I embrace it. I am able to use it when I get to a place of my own inner reflection. When I am able to realize my need for others and their need for me, it is much easier to ask for help and much easier to accept it.

I stand open and willing.

Commitment, Willingness, and Surrender

Breaking old patterns, getting out of comfort zones, getting out of the way of all your old "stuff" that kept you in *no* and hiding from your *Yes*—all go much easier if you remember:

- Love may look past your addictions, but it may also make it easy for you to stay in your comfort zone
- Committed love, on the other hand, will see you through
- To be willing, you may have to struggle with your belief system and/or your will—which may be ego-driven.
- An intermediate step of being willing to surrender to a Higher Power as you see it or surrendering the outcome may help
- Rugged individualism may stand in the way of recovery and willingness
- Helpless dependency on others keeps you away from *Yes*.
- Interdependent cooperation can get you where you need to be
- Surrendering to a Higher Power paradoxically increases your own power

This third key, having the willingness and courage to step out of comfort zones and hiding places, is the biggest and most challenging of the five steps. The fourth step will go within and allow time for *Yes* to take shape. The fifth step will be about taking action to let things happen, and in chapter ten we'll be looking at willingness again, the willingness to take creative risks.

CHAPTER 8

As Much Time
As It Takes

I can't count how often I've heard: "Take your time…Wait for the right time…Good things take time." These phrases all ask me to tap into my patience. But I am not patient. Substance abusers are not at all patient people. In fact, as a group, they could be the most impatient bunch around.

Here is a real example of an addict's impatience: It takes more time for cocaine to reach the brain and give the high when you snort than it does to smoke it, and even less time when we free base or inject it. So, freebasing and injecting end up being the preferred option for addicts. How much time is involved? What's the difference in the effect time? About five seconds. But a true cocaine addict wants the high right now, not in a few seconds. Nike's slogan, "Just Do It," may be aimed at weekend warriors, but coke addicts have been using that as a mantra since way before Nike took it up.

Impatience Is a Gift

Addicts may have positive character traits, but patience is not one of them. I was never patient. I may be clean and sober now, but clean and sober does not always mean clean and patient. I am still impatient. My temperament and skills set do not always mesh with the many bureaucratic issues I deal with as the executive director of a multi-million-dollar non-profit agency. Piles and piles of paper work, endless forms, and regulations all delay delivering care to the folks who need it most. The larger the agency becomes, the more decision-makers are involved and the more time it takes to actually make a decision.

My impatience has gotten me into trouble with my board, my family, my life. I have been known to send ten emails to an individual within a twenty-minute time period or call numerous persons about the same topic within an hour as I try to nail down an answer. Impatience gets things done if you can sit and wait. To sit and wait is not a part of my cell structure. Sit and wait was given to someone else, not me.

My impatience is a gift; I believe this. For me, "do it now" has always described everything I do. Being impatient makes things happen. Not always good things, but things happen, and there is no long, drawn-out waiting period. Hell for me will be a waiting room. Of course, when I make call after call to my board, ask Michelle the same question again and again in the hope of speeding up her answer, or when I jump into a situation without looking at what could go wrong, I can sometimes create issues. There have been days when I felt as if the Universe had a giant two-by-four that it kept swinging so I would pay attention and wait. Maybe I have been hit enough or maybe it is because I have actually acquired a little wisdom after fifty-four years. Some of the time I do realize that waiting for the right time, waiting for a better answer, or waiting to ask can be as helpful as *right now* impatience.

I often have to slow my brain down as it jumps from project to project to keep it from anticipating catastrophic outcomes. It's probably a carryover from the daily pessimism of my youth that I tend to be a "glass is half empty" kind of person. I'm still working on reining in my pessimistic thoughts when they take off like horses at the Kentucky Derby when I am waiting for a decision from someone or waiting for the results of a survey or bid. I just *know* the outcome will be bad.

This is undoubtedly one main reason why I hate waiting. I hate the thoughts racing around and around on the well-worn track inside of my brain. Before I can talk myself out of it, I am on the phone calling to ask, *"What is taking so friggin' long?"* My anxiety builds when I am placed on hold, and my thoughts tell me the news will not be to my liking. When I am told it will take another week or even another hour, my impatience screams at me to do something. And that is just what I am like today. Trust me; I was much worse before 1984. Much, much worse. Each and every day I get better. I will hang on to the impatient side of me that makes sh** happen even while I nurture the small, patient part of me who has more trust and more faith that the glass just might be half full.

Finding Patience

I know recovery demands patience. I even tell others to be patient. Yet, when I think of all that is left to be done, all the people who still need jobs, homes, and hope, my impatience gets me back on the phone and back to the emails. Recovery demands that you trust the process. So, I wait, and I trust. While I am waiting, I pray or I begin a new project. Recovery demands that you take time for priorities.

In the past if I didn't get results immediately I'd move on, which conflicts with what is needed for sobriety and certainly for lasting relationships. Because I'm committed to sobriety, committed to relationships, I now take the time.

I am beginning to understand that this Higher Power wants me to take it one day at a time in all areas of life, and, while I am at it, to trust. Trust that what I have put in motion will complete itself without my endless emails and phone calls to just check up and check in. Trust that something bigger than

Scott H. Silverman is going on. Trust that if I take the time to do my part, the Higher Power will do His (or Her) part.

What amazes me is that I *can* wait, I *am* able to trust (a little more) and I *have* been able to restrain the part of me that wants to push rather than lead a project. What really amazes me is that I've learned to spend the waiting time productively. The project gets completed, I find places deep within that have stretched, and I have more certainty. And with certainty comes more trust.

You're Always Learning

Most of my life I have done whatever it took to get what I wanted. It is unfortunate that for part of my life what I wanted, or thought I wanted, was devastation. Nevertheless, some of what I wanted during my drug years actually benefited me. Once we decide to get out of our comfort zones, find our *Yes*, and change, all our experiences can be used.

I started out just wanting to be good at something, so good that I would banish the name-calling, the disappointment of teachers and parents and earn affection, admiration, and respect. When I couldn't do this easily, I gave up on *Yes* and became so good at living in *no* that I became an award-winning member of the exclusive *Le Turd* club. Many addicts envision grand accomplishment to offset their shame. When I was first in recovery, I couldn't even fly kites without aspiring to be the best kite-flyer in the county. I lived kites morning, noon, and, night and I took the kites on vacation with me, even on the plane. My obsessive grandiosity became a powerful vision when I combined it with *Yes*. I dream big, and once I discovered the five keys, I found a lot to show for my obsession.

During my years of non-productive, non-profitable drinking, drugging, making an ass of myself, lying, conniving, and rebelling, I dove into the addiction pool without checking to see how deep the water really was. I always dove. Never would I tiptoe.

You are either in, or you are out. I want to live fully involved, always. But going overboard, even while it is potentially reckless, has a positive side, as I began to discover. Once I made the choice to believe that my life was worth living and worth living well, I committed fully to recovery, attending over a hundred twelve-step meetings in ninety days. Today I help my people get back on their feet—a project I now dive into with one hundred percent exuberance. Maybe I'm obsessed; maybe I just keep trading the addictions. I don't know. However, I have to work with what I have. My intensity, my propensity to jump in with both feet, allows the passion that lives inside of me to emerge, moves me through the *no's,* gets me to *Yes,* and takes others along when I jump.

Somewhere during my years of using, I learned to charm my way in and out of situations. That charm has proved vital in fundraising. When I was in the Middle East and Europe, I learned that when a discomfort—like crating chickens—is too great, I can walk away; I learned that I could endure a lot—cold, grueling labor, chicken shit—before I reach the quitting place. I learned to stand on my own and to get around obstacles. I learned not to trust everybody who smiled at me. Most of all, I learned that wherever I go, there are always ways to get what I want or need. I learned to be resourceful.

Turkey especially taught me that people will do whatever it takes to survive. This continues to help me with my clients today, as it keeps me from judging and from being naive. I also learned that I love living on the edge, scrambling when times get tough. Even learning what good hashish was served me entrepreneurially in Amsterdam and later. All of this would be useful in the first years of setting up Second Chance. Nothing we do is wasted. Nothing.

In taking time to find and nurture your *Yes,* don't spend your time kicking yourself for past mistakes and character flaws.

Instead, appreciate all that you've learned from your struggles. You have discovered the pluses and minuses of your basic nature and learned how to put them to work for you.

Caring

Addicts spend a great deal of time with distraction. They have little time for family and only small amounts of time for education or career. Yet they have unlimited hours to explore new and creative ways to distract themselves from a world they blame on others. I spent my time as an addict creating distance from pain and embarrassment. Before my recovery, I would tell people that I had no time, no way, to do everything I had on my calendar.

No one changes completely or overnight. My days of distracting myself through drinking and drugging were over, but I didn't just one day say, "Done!" and become a different person. I beat the drugs and liquid tranquility only to find the joy of chain smoking. I used one cigarette to light the next, and my energy and fear of what might be inside of me relaxed a bit. Dulling my brain, my emotions, and my experiences with nicotine helped me grow strong enough to admit how much I cared about what I saw happening in the world. I'd spent my drug years trying to convince myself that I didn't care about much of anything, deadening all my caring impulses. And then, there those impulses were, alive and screaming. Have you ever experienced the pain of allowing caring to run your life? I have.

Cigarettes helped for a time. Then I had to stop those or die. What came next? The drugs were gone, the booze was gone, the cigarettes were gone. What was left? Food. Lots and lots and lots of food. Lonely? Eat. Tired? Eat. Angry? Eat. Tastes good? Eat. I ate until I began to look more like a marshmallow than a man. It was tough to stop eating. I did liquid diets, fiber diets, carb diets, protein diets, soup diets, the "you name it, I did it" diet. I lost pounds but I still hadn't lost the urge to hide the feelings and distract myself from caring.

No one will ever tell me I am moderate. I am extreme. And I kinda like extreme, but at 322 pounds, I was an extreme that even I found too extreme, and I could see a future of 350 looming. I had to act. Many believe that weight is about will power, and it may well be. My will power was jump-started with a gastric bypass procedure. Extreme? I guess so, but so is death by obesity. Gastric bypass surgery guarantees you can only eat small amounts of food at one sitting, and these foods need to be nutritious. The surgery not only provided the tool I needed to stop eating dinners planned for a family of four, it also provided a way to stop stuffing emotions, energy, and passion down my throat with a couple of Big Macs. Comfort food was no longer an option, and I was forced to find inner comfort, creative comfort.

So, now that I couldn't stuff my caring, energy, and passion, what did I do with it? I channeled it into *Yes* and then into Second Chance. Twenty-some years later, the time available to me seems to have doubled. I am doing twice as much as before. Perhaps there is some warp in the Universe that has doubled the time I have every day. What I've done is to simply cut out the time I spend distracting myself from caring.

Regret

Another common theme in an addict's repitoire is regret. They regret, and they remind themselves, "Nothing I can do about it, right? The world is against screwed up people. I cannot figure it out, and there is nothing I can do. " They keep the self-pity valve open, and guess where that pity leads—to a predictable relapse.

Misspent time is a common source of regret. It's tempting and fascinating to think how many "ifs" live inside a person's life. *If* I had been working in a different industry; *if* I had not joined the family business; *if* the media people hadn't encouraged my addictions; *if* I had been arrested in New York and not taken back to the hotel; *if, if, if.* The *ifs* live in everyone's life. All the ifs are like toggles set in a particular sequence to open some doors and close others. They ultimately determine the path everyone follows. Yet when addicts think along these lines, they often wallow in excuses and self-pity and segue into relapse.

I know this so well. I try to let go of most of most of my regrets. If you have a regret you just can't dismiss, you need to spend time taking a long and thoughtful look at it. My biggest regret is about my time with Gregg. His story holds a powerful gift for me, yet I'd give anything to have a do-over.

My Brother Gregg

My sister Marsi was four and I was two when my parents brought home someone they called Gregg Paul Silverman. He cried and took up the room in my mother's arms that had been mine. My parents put him in my room. I was surprised, as I had not asked for a Gregg Paul Silverman or for a baby. I was a baby, and I didn't want to have any more than one of me. I waited for them to take him back to wherever they had gotten him, but it seemed he was going to stay. With me. In my room.

We had recently moved into a home on Mt. Helix, in La Mesa, California. Mt. Helix is about twenty minutes from downtown San Diego and a short drive to my parents' stores in El Cajon. This was the California of orange groves, lemon trees, and avocado orchards. It is still a unique area of Southern California with its curvy, quiet, private roads, clean, unpretentious homes with serious acreage, and not a sidewalk anywhere. This would be my home for the next eleven years and offer me the freedom to explore, climb trees, and build my tree house. A young boy's dream! But there was one drawback: not enough bedrooms, so my new little brother and I shared a room.

Two people could never be so different. He was good, I was bad. I rebelled, he went along. I had no grasp of numbers, letters and rules; he was honor roll. In third grade, Gregg was creating paintings that people framed. I was using my hands to build forts, hideaways, and tree houses. Every day, I looked around the family I had been born into and decided that I was a freak. I could get it that Marsi and Stacy (born two years after Gregg) were different, smarter, and responsible. They made my parents smile. They were girls. What I couldn't get was that Gregg, a boy for God's sake, also made my parents smile. Gregg proved that it was I who was wrong and that the family I loved was disappointed in who I was. No one said it—no one needed to. There was Gregg, shining, achieving, popular, and then there was me. He was growing into this stellar kid. I was growing madder.

Kids fight. Gregg and I battled. The emergency room staff got to know us. Stitches, cuts, scrapes, bloody noses. The time I spent at school proved to me that I was wrong, stupid, and unacceptable. The time I spent at home proved to me that I was an angry, rebellious black sheep. Whenever I could, I spent time outdoors, kicking balls, throwing balls, hitting balls. I rode my bike, climbed trees, stole avocadoes from neighbors, and picked lemons to make into lemonade. During a peaceful stretch, Gregg and I joined together to set up a stand and sell what we picked and what we made. Even then, I did not see that I shared entrepreneurship with Gregg. I did not see that I shared creativity with Gregg. I did not see that I shared love with Gregg. I only saw the differences, and I judged myself by those differences and in my young mind, I came up wanting.

Eventually, we moved from Mt. Helix to a more central location. I got my own room, and the fights grew less and less. I spent my time with Tom then, and a few others who shared my lifelong love of rule-breaking and my newfound love of drinking. I grew older and created a world far from the people with whom I lived. I may have shared space with Gregg, Marsi, Stacy, and my parents, but I did not share their world. I knew they saw me as stupid, and I decided they were educational snobs. I made sure not to spend my time with them. I determined to spend my time creating an intimacy with distraction, distancing myself from caring that my family doted on Gregg but was not pleased with me.

I wish I had spent more time getting to know that gifted boy, the amazing teen who was liked by everyone; the tuxedo-clad, corsage-in-hand young man who escorted my Michelle to her prom. I wish I'd had real conversations with him and befriended the brain who started businesses years ahead of his competition. Instead, I judged him and I judged myself when I was with him. I always came up short, and so I stayed away. I could have learned from him, and I hope he could have learned from me.

In 1986, Gregg let us know that he had been diagnosed with a disease called ARC. The doctors told us that ARC was an incurable disease. He developed sores on his face that would not clear up. All I could do was watch Gregg fade. No longer a sought-after man of vision and art, he was shunned—not by his family, but by society. He gave up his home in San Francisco, moved closer to us (to L.A.), and began an unending round of hospital stays between hopeful days at home. He shared a floor of the hospital with a few others; the floor had been named after the disease they were all battling. The disease now carried the name AIDS.

In the 1980s, AIDS equaled leprosy. Gregg's floor was a ward of isolation. Many of the young men there had no family who would ever visit them. Most of these men died alone, never sharing who they were with those who raised them. The sadness of that time was staggering.

Gregg died at home. His lover, my sisters, their husbands, Michelle, and I gathered with my parents as he left his body. As we prepared for a funeral and memorial service, we read the eulogy Gregg had written for himself. He knew he was going to die, and he wanted certain words said and particular points made. He even asked that a friend from his camp days officiate the service. She was our Rabbi at the time and was honored to lead the service.

To say my mother was devastated would be an understatement. To lose a son is not the natural order of life, but then again Mom had never really been dealt the hand that was the natural order. She wanted to underplay that Gregg was gay and he died of AIDS. Why subject our family and Gregg's memory to gossip or ridicule? Our Jewish community had no gays and certainly no deaths from an incurable and unspoken disease. The less said the better. Even in death, her wish was to protect her son. The rest of us thought otherwise. Our family became the first Jewish family in our area to speak out and declare that we had a gay son, a gay brother, and that AIDS had taken his life. Gregg became the *Yes* for a community of gay Jewish individuals without ever knowing it. It's remarkable what happens when *Yes* directs and truth leads. My mother joined us. She became the go-to person for Jewish families struggling with AIDS, gay children, grief, anger, and the challenge of moving forward. To this day, Maggie Silverman is contacted when a diagnosis is shared or when young men and women in our community come out and state, "I'm gay."

Transcending Regret

The regrets I felt following Gregg's death made me sick. Yet, those regrets helped me decide how I would spend the time I had left in my life. I regretted the lost time with Gregg. I regretted the lost time I spent trying to kill myself with substances, thoughts, and actions. I regretted the lost time I spent ignoring the life, the gift, I had been given. I swore to myself that from then on I would treat every person I met as if they were a gift in my life. I swore to myself to be available to any and all opportunities that could lift humanity and never to degrade it. I swore to myself that when I said goodbye to my family, my friends, my cherished Michelle, my daughters, Gracie and Jessica, and everyone else, I would feel as if I had really used the time given to me. I would have known those I loved and they would have known me. I would have dedicated every twenty-four hour allotment to whatever higher plan my Higher Power had for me.

Gregg's illness and death changed our family. Forever. Perhaps I would have come to my decisions without his illness and early death. I do know that dealing with AIDS and the stigmas that go with it propelled me. The death of my brother slingshot me forward to a deeper commitment to life. I like to believe that Gregg was one of many who gave their life so others could live more freely, more openly. I like to believe Gregg can see us gather on Friday at sundown or during High Holidays and that he can hear us toast him as the hero he will always be. It's so good to have a hero.

Heroes help us transform regret into positive new goals to correct or improve whatever situation the hero battles. To varying degrees, we all become champions of his or her cause. Following a hero as a role model can transform all the self-torture over misspent time by showing us the way to compensate through helping others, paying-it-forward, and giving back. The inspiration of a hero can help deflect a harsh reality and provide a focus for deep down caring. Heroes allow us to glimpse our own inner hero.

Solitude

In my early days of recovery, someone gave me an assignment to take a three-hour walk. My response was, "What if I get bored?" They had a great come back, "Consider the company you are keeping!"

Despite my loner childhood, spending time alone now makes me uncomfortable. But I know I need to do it. I'm no longer stuck in comfort zones. I might enjoy them, but I'm not locked inside them. I know I must schedule time to be alone with just my thoughts and my emotions. I need to schedule that time to face whatever needs to shift for me to grow into the next manifestation of me.

As a boy, I had no trouble spending hours and hours and hours alone. There was my tree house, walks in the woods, and adventures with my bow and arrow. How could I be so alone with myself in childhood, while at fifty-four I feel scared when I think about spending time without a computer or phone or someone else to focus on? That fear keeps me humble. I know I continue to be in the process of *Yes*. My prayer—no, my belief—is that there will be a day when I can just take off, like little Scotty did over forty-five years ago, with only a sandwich and my thoughts and actually look forward to it. It is what my *Yes* is now asking. Will I take the time to be with my deeper self? Am I willing to commit to time alone to find what is waiting for me?

One thing I am certain of—*Yes* demands time. No shortcuts. My life today is structured, moment to moment, and my time is devoted to others. For me to grow and for my vision to expand, my life must change again. I must take the time. I am willing.

Your Day, Your Time

In the process of allowing time to work its magic for you, don't wait for someone else to act. It is your day, your time. Use it. Now.

- Recovery demands time and therefore patience
- Addicts tend not to be patient, so this step can be a challenge
- Learning to trust builds patience, which builds more trust, which nourishes patience and more trust…
- Many addicts can redirect their traits into positive energy once they partner with *Yes*
- Impatience can be redirected into productivity and accomplishment
- Experiences are valuable, and nothing is wasted
- Even regret can become a powerful engine behind positive goals and accomplishments
- Embracing solitude is like breathing fresh air and helps build your *Yes*

Once you've worked your way through these first four keys, you're in for the most exciting part of the journey, because in the fifth step, *Yes* will be your inspiration as you translate it into action.

CHAPTER 9

Persevere: There Is Always a Way

"Tell Me No, I Dare You" is not just a motto I use with others. It is the song I sing to myself. I want the good outcome, the happy ending.

At times, you may believe happy endings are too uncertain, too iffy, or too hard to conceive of. The obstacles are too firm to move, or the odds are too stacked against success. But in spite of the challenges that block our desires, I believe we are well equipped to find a way to have the happy ending we want, to get the outcome we set out to achieve. In fact, I believe we can get what we set out to achieve or possibly—and it happens from time to time—we get something better.

Every once in a while I'll read something in a book or newspaper that resonates a major truth for me, and I will write it out and use it as a motivation. In several different publications, in slightly various forms, Henry Ford has been quoted as saying, basically, "If you think you will fail, you are right; and if you think you will succeed, you are right." I have decided to choose to succeed.

As I moved through twelve-step work, gang eradication assignments, financial failures, and even bankruptcy, I had an inner knowing, an inner voice, an inner *Yes*. I not only knew I would survive, I knew I would do something with my life. I realize now that knew this when I was a teenager living in Tucson and going to a school I hated. I knew I would do something with my life even when teachers, counselors, psychologists, and job development hotshots told me I wouldn't. I even knew that there was a better life when I was ready to drop forty-four flights to the New York pavement. Some part of me, the part I call my *Yes* part, knew that Second Chance was waiting to be started, and it was waiting for me to start it. By the time I began helping the homeless, the ex-felons, and the drug addicted people living in San Diego, I knew what discomfort felt like, and I was willing to take it on and commit to turning my dream into reality.

Everyone has an inner *Yes.* How does it materialize into the world?

Vision

How did my commitment to help others translate into an almost four-million dollar not-for-profit agency? I set everything in motion, and it developed from there. To give back, I decided I needed to volunteer at the hospital where I received treatment. I volunteered 4,000 hours at Sharp Memorial Hospital and also at St. Vincent DePaul, a charitable organization that helps those down on their luck. I watched TV when I couldn't sleep to let the mindless, distracting chatter keep my mind off drugs.

There was one infomercial on late-night TV about buying a house with a credit card. I was committed to my family, including the commitment to supporting them. I watched the informercial and I suddenly had a direction. I would invest in real estate. I used my credit card to make the down payment on a duplex. This was during the mid 1980s when crack was moving into San Diego. My first tenant came with a reference from a previous landlord. The reference didn't mention that my new tenant was a drug dealer who would quickly open up shop in what was my first real estate investment. This new development seemed to me to be a huge *no*. *"Tell Me No, I Dare You"* kicked in, and I called the previous landlord who had sent me the recommendation for my drug dealer.

"What the hell?" I am not one to try diplomacy, and besides, my future was on the line. I wanted an answer from this landlord, and I wanted to know how to get back to *Yes*.

"I'm sorry," he said. "I kept trying to get rid of him, and I figured if you took him I would be rid of him and the drug dealing. Now I have other ones trying to move in."

I could have responded in anger, but I was committed to finding a solution. I got on the phone and began to call other landlords in the San Diego area. It didn't take me long to discover drugs had become an epidemic, and no one was breaking up the dealers. It would be nice to think I organized the landlords to help save those addicted to drugs. But the truth is, I organized landlords to save my investment. I told them that if they would pay me, I would get the drug dealers out and collect the rents. They jumped at the idea.

From my days of scrambling among drug dealers, I had an idea of how to go about this task. I put on a flak jacket (bullet-proof vest) and outfitted myself with a Sig Sauer. Wearing level four body armor, I started knocking on doors. When I used drugs, there were no slogans, no "Just Say No" campaigns, for me to defy. I was now clean and sober, and times had changed. This was during the time of President Reagan's "Just Say No" campaign. I could tell which places were selling drugs: they were the ones with "Just Say No" signs on their doors and windows. I knew defiance when I saw it! Here I was a nice Jewish boy from La Jolla, California, with a flak jacket and guns, and I was actually breaking up gangs! Guns were powerful persuaders.

I remember one incident when I knocked on the door of some druggie who was not paying his rent to tell him he needed to pay or go. This huge black man with arms as big as my legs grabbed me by my shirt, and as he pulled me forward, he put a knife to my throat. "Now, what are ya gonna do, Honkey?"

Excellent question!

What I was did was pull out my Sig Sauer 9mm, let him see it, and have him take the knife away from my just-shaved skin. It worked just like I thought it would. His question had a great answer! Word spread, and I was given more work. I met with good tenants and bad tenants. I met with hoodlums and knuckleheads and all sorts of individuals who were getting evicted. It was obvious that rent money was going to drugs and that drugs were being dealt out of the back windows and doorways.

It is amazing what crack and meth addictions and other abuses get people to do. Some of the apartments had huge holes in the walls. The holes were not caused by fights or drunkenness; they were the result of deliberate cutting into the drywall. Drugs cost money, and behind the drywall were copper pipes the addicts could sell to get drug money. How much could they get for copper pipe? Not much, but it was enough to score again. Addicts have perseverance, creativity, and determination. They are misplaced, but they are there.

My job was to go in and eradicate the drug problem. I helped some people hook up with the Housing Commission and into twelve-step programs. The commission would help with the rent, and the twelve-step program would help with the drug problem. I was acting on the commitment I had made to help others. The help was working, and progress was being made. An added benefit was that as I helped others, I helped myself.

I continued to volunteer at my temple on Sundays and at St. Vincent DePaul to support our temple's Hunger Project. As I volunteered at these places, I started noticing something curious:

of the eight hundred people who showed up for breakfast, I would know four hundred of them from the work I had done through the Housing Commission and rehab center. I started asking questions.

"Why aren't you working? How are you going to pay rent if you don't have a job?" I saw that a lot of the work I had done to help them had gone down the drain. At the very least, I could see I would once again have to repeat getting them help with their rent. Something had to change, and I needed to know what was keeping them from working. The answers varied.

"I've got a record."

"I'm an ex-offender."

"I have substance abuse and a sketchy work record in my past."

"No one is going to hire me."

I listened to the same sorry stories for about six months and decided I could do something about it. I began to network with nonprofit social agencies: Good Will, Volunteers of America, Salvation Army, Police Services, and of course, St. Vincent DePaul. I met with directors, deployment specialists, and job handlers at these organizations. I told them I could get housing and jobs for their clients. I was direct and let them know that I was a for-profit venture and would partner with them. I could fill the rentals I owned to capacity. I needed them only to buy beds.

They all loved the idea and told me they would get back to me at the end of the quarter. I was very enthusiastic about this plan. Not only would it help people get jobs, it would help the landlords, such as myself, begin to fill their rentals. But, it was a bad time for the U.S. economy. Savings and loans were failing, the real estate market was not in good shape, and I was not the only one facing financial challenges.

I gave presentations to nonprofit agencies about providing

jobs and housing, residential treatment, and health care. "I want to do this to help people gain employment," I told them. I knew it was possible. If I could help these people get started and clean up their credit, eventually they could own their own home. I knew they could make a better life. I was certain I would get the agencies behind me. Why not? Everybody would win!

The agencies voted unanimously *not* to work with me.

They were quick to assure me they loved my enthusiasm and the philosophy behind my presentation, but they were worried about would happen if my plan was a success. "If you are successful, Scott, what will we do? We will be out of jobs. We appreciate you coming down and sharing your vision, and we wish you luck." They were not worried about my plan failing, they were worried about it *succeeding*!

To say I was upset is an understatement. I went home that afternoon with one of the worst cases of f*** it I have possibly ever had. Yet I still wanted to do this. I could see the *Yes,* even if others were afraid. I knew it was possible. My commitment to help others had taken me to my next *Yes.* Second Chance was born out of that rejection. My commitment to helping others now became my career. I went to the library and asked for a book on how to start a nonprofit. My life was about to change again.

Swimming the English Channel

Liking to be with people is not the same as working with people. Working with an advisory board and not being my accustomed lone wolf required me to sacrifice comfort. I had committed myself to a vision that came to me: seeing the homeless in homes, the druggies in self-respect and responsible work, and ex-offenders giving back to the society from which they once took. That was and is the vision for which I am willing to be uncomfortable.

The first year of building Second Chance was like announcing an intention to swim the English Channel and then jumping into water over my head without knowing how to swim. I was tossed around like a beach ball in a storm. It felt as if I were eddying in circles for most of that first year. I was learning every day, but painful lessons came when doors were slammed and rejections piled up. I was growing a very thick skin from the broken promises, misguided trust, and buffeting between confusion, frustration, and determination.

The entire adventure bounced from exhilarating whenever agreements were signed or promises actually came through to utterly deflating when I didn't get funding because someone changed their mind. I went through an emotional wringer. It got to the point where it seemed like I took one step forward and slid two or three or four steps back. I sweated a lot during those days, and not from cocaine. But I was learning how to become more resilient. This time, my resiliency was directed toward positive effects, not damaging behavior.

My wounds healed and my skin grew tough. I was persistent. I was driven. And always, I felt the personal responsibility I had been given as an addict who survived and turned the big corner.

The Discomfort Zone

The second year was not much better. I re-prioritized my time and efforts to focus on learning without pain. What a concept! I spent hundreds of hours gathering information on nonprofits, advisory boards, and governing bodies. I was exposed to words that I had never heard. Bylaw? When I first saw that word, I actually thought it was some type of law that governed gays and straights! Looking back, it was time well spent. Yet I expended all this time and all this effort, and I still was not making a dime. It was obvious that I needed to go out and raise money.

My vision kept me going. I set out to get a few of the goofs off the street, into a home, and working at jobs that could go somewhere. I found a way that I really believed would be possible, and I knew it would be a cinch to convince others to help me do this. So, with my vision clearly in my mind, I set out to make it a reality.

Raising money is an art. The number one reason people donate money is not the cause, and it is has little to do with bonus gifts. The number one reason people donate money is because they are asked to. I asked and asked and asked. I got substantially more no's than yeses. I could never predict where the money would come from. At first, I approached everyone with confidence, because, after all, this was such an extraordinary opportunity to change the whole damn world! How could or why would anyone say no? It didn't take long before I revised my thinking. I discovered that fund raising was very uncertain and unpredictable.

My family members were my first goal, and as expected, they were completely supportive; they saw what I saw. They got it. They lovingly gave me money to get started in this honorable, charitable work. Some friends pitched in as well; they saw the sincere effort I was making to help out our little world in San Diego. I asked my congregation, and I asked my club members. Eventually I got some yeses. I kept asking because I could see what was possible. I knew I could get people off of the streets and into jobs. I knew there was an answer, and that answer had absolutely nothing to do with *no* and everything to do with *Yes*. The *Yes* I felt about Second Chance focused my attention and my time. I was willing to be very uncomfortable to get what I knew was available. I still am.

There is nothing comfortable about applying for non-profit status. It is a very complex process. I filled out paper after paper and finally completed every step, only to be told it would take about a year to get the coveted status. That was absolutely *not* going to work. I made telephone call after telephone call and eventually found a woman who told me the same story as everyone else. I explained to her how I really needed the okay sooner. I was trying to do the one-day-at-a-time thing, but it was getting tough.

"One day at a time? Are you a friend of Bill W.?"

Bill W. is the genius responsible for starting the twelve-step movement. The woman was asking if I was in a twelve-step program.

"I definitely am!" I responded. I had my nonprofit status within a month. It pays to persevere and to be honest. It also doesn't hurt to have connections!

Turning *No* into *Yes*

At last, Second Chance was born. I got enough money together to buy a hotel where we could house our clients. I'd found a rattrap of a building filled with dog shit. I cleaned it and turned it into an office and training space. None of this was easy; most of it created an enormous amount of discomfort. Yet I knew I was doing it for a reason, and that made the pain bearable.

It made perfect sense to me that if the guy on the corner who needed to eat and survive had a job, paid rent, and had a place to go to at the end of the day, if he had all of that, he'd have no need to take my wallet. It made perfect sense to me that if we raised the money to create a way for an ex-felon to live in a safe house, discover what he was good at that was actually productive, we might keep him out of the endless cycle of prison, re-arrest, prison, and re-arrest. It would certainly be cheaper than spending $44,000 a year to keep him locked up. I'd get the goofs off the street and turn them into positive contributors. Everybody would win, I still believed that people would be delighted to support it with their donations.

I'd already purchased a safe house, but I needed help buying beds, paying rent, assembling and training a staff, getting equipment and supplies, and paying for the typical expenses of running a business. With such a win/win venture, I went out into the community and involved the public at large.

Much to my amazement, the people I was certain would contribute, the movers and shakers whose businesses would be most greatly enhanced by the conversion of these goofs, all said "No, thanks."

I was puzzled. I was stunned. I was incredulous. But, I was not at all deterred. I decided to ask them again and explain in greater detail the benefits of donating to my worthy cause. I concluded that I must not have conveyed my message sufficiently during the initial introduction. This time, I would paint a clearer picture, a rosier view of the benefits to them and to society as a whole. This time, their response would be different!

It was. This time, their response was *no* with a capital N and a capital O. Did I understand? Yes, I heard. Yes, I understood. I was setting up this noble non-profit, filling out pages of applications, answering seemingly endless series of questionnaires, all while trying to help support a wife and two little girls. I promised people I'd get them work. I had made commitments to people. Where would they live while I was teaching them interview skills? How could I deliver what I had promised? I had rented a broken down building to house us so we could start the simple process. And the word I kept hearing from the community was "No!"

But underneath all the *no's*, the soft, steady word I listened to and repeated to myself was *Yes!* I could tell, though, that this *Yes* was going to take some outside-the-box thinking. More than a few people thought I was nuts. Why would I do something like this and how could I support a family when I never knew if I had any money?

I stayed with it and I used the *no's* I heard to reach out to a broader group of people—people I might never have otherwise called or met. I used the charm that had served me so well in my drug days, and I found I still had it. Lo and behold, I started to raise money. Then I raised more money. People responded to my concept, just as I knew they would from the beginning. It required time and persistence. It took stamina and commitment and the willingness to ask until I got the answer I wanted. It wasn't easy. It wasn't without much frustration and disappointment and rejection. But the money came.

For the first ten years of Second Chance, we relied strictly on private donations. Eventually, some donors introduced me to political leaders, decision makers, and bigger donors. We recently received a check from a senator for close to $700,000, which was a godsend, even though we had to wait for the check to clear to cover our payroll, because payroll is a bit bigger these days!

If I could do this without a college education and with a brain that had been bombarded by drugs and alcohol for decades, anyone can do it or something like it. What I needed to keep in mind is that I will always find a way. Always.

"The way" may compel me to get creative. This step is so important I will devote a separate chapter to it.

Remember:

- Focus on your commitment to your vision and start moving in that direction
- You may need to "just do it" and take the plunge
- Become very resilient
- Be willing to endure the discomfort zone
- Stay focused on your vision, on your determination, and on your *Yes*
- Don't accept *no*
- Believe that there is always a way—always

CHAPTER 10

Creativity

In the movie *Million Dollar Baby*, there is a poster on the wall in the gym where Clint Eastwood's character trains Hillary Swank's character. It is not prominent, but I noticed it right away in the background in a couple of shots. It grabbed my attention because it sums up what I teach and how I try to live. The poster simply reads, "Winners are willing to do what losers are not." I cannot imagine anything more true in this world.

What is a winner? Does the love of competition create a winner? Does losing mean you come in last or that you just don't even flipping try?

Winning individuals are driven from deep in their gut. Winners are individuals who are successful at whatever they attempt, even if the success is the decision to get out. If there is one significant distinction between those who succeed and those who do not, it is summed up in that poster. *Winners are willing to do what losers are not.* There is a tremendously profound truth in that simple statement. If I want something—sobriety, a good marriage, a growing agency, even a better hotel room—I have to be willing to do what it takes. I have to be willing to deal with the barriers and to know that there is a way *even if I do not immediately see it.*

If I do not believe there is a way, I am right. Remember what

Henry Ford said. If I believe there is a way, I am also right. My brain has—all of our brains have—the creative potential to work around any barriers. The question we must answer is "Am I willing?…Am I willing to do *whatever* it takes to get what my heart tells me is possible?" If you are not willing to do what it takes, I say, "Don't do it!" If you are, you can, metaphorically, leap into the English Channel for a marathon swim.

There Is No Frickin' Box

To get from Point A (my starting point) to Point Z (my ultimate goal), I am always willing to do what the other guy won't do, as long as it is legal and does not cause harm. While I keep Point Z in my mind, I continually search for Point B, then Point C, then Point D. That's the only way I know to get to Point Z.

Let's get started. Let's get out of the board rooms, the meeting rooms, and the news shows, and let's frickin' get started. Doing what it takes, believing a way will open, and knowing that your brain has the potential to solve problems and create change grows out of the experience of doing. You finish a march by placing one foot in front of the other, whether that march is to assure all children are granted equal education, to spearhead a movement for better health, or to repair a broken faucet. You'll never find the way if you are lying on the couch or complaining about the cost of gasoline.

There are hundreds and hundreds of examples of the power of action, trust, and creativity. Inventions, medical discoveries, and even social change confirm this. Someone is appalled at the condition of a road that thousands drive on daily and cannot rest until the pot holes, crumbling surface, and jagged shoulders are repaired. Calls are made, newspapers contacted, petitions signed…and the road gets fixed. Another hero decides it is no longer tolerable for courts to look the other way as one more drunk driver gets the car keys back.

"That's the way it is always done."

"Can't fight city hall."

"No one is going to help you."

"Everyone has driven after they have had a few drinks."

These are all the things people may hear while their gut keeps telling them, "This is not right!" So *one* person begins to call others, sits in all the courtrooms where there drunk driver cases are heard, sends thousands of letters, and changes the laws—*one* person who believes that it can be done and one person who is willing to *take action* on that belief. One person who doesn't just think outside the box, but dismantles it.

I am all for dismantling the box. Take it apart, and, if you need to, put it back together with more room inside. The funny part is, if you dismantle this box enough times, you begin to realize there is no frickin' box, except in your mind.

Working with Others

I am highly motivated to find any business that Second Chance can run profitably and which will also employ a good number of our graduates. In 1993, when we were first starting Second Chance, I heard that Ben & Jerry's Ice Cream would partner with non-profits. I didn't contact them right away. Back then, I didn't know how many people we would need to place, how much money we would need, or even how long I would be doing this non-profit gig. I had my intention to get some guys off the street and teach them a few skills before I got involved in any kind of "real" business. I finally did contact Ben & Jerry's ten years later, in 2003. Ben and Jerry were still willing to partner with non-profits. I thought it would be a great fit. It was an ideal business: it did not serve alcohol, personnel needed a relatively small amount of training, and it could be profitable quickly and help Second Chance pay the bills while we placed graduates into jobs with a future.

The application arrived. I filled out reams of paper, a lot of paperwork, in fact, for a guy who did not learn to read until he was in fourth grade. Then we waited. Patience and waiting were still not concepts I found appealing. Even when there is only one person in front of me in the grocery store line, my reaction is, "Oh, no! There's a frickin' line!" But, what could I do except be patient? So I waited. The due diligence took about six months; then Ben & Jerry's said, "No."

Now that inspired me! Instead of just accepting the "no," I took action. I went to Vermont to visit the black and white cows and Ben & Jerry. They told me the reason why Second Chance was rejected was that Ben & Jerry's was committed to empowering youth and Second Chance did not deal with enough youth in our clientele.

"How many youth do you want us to serve?" Their answer was, "At least 25% of your clients."

We served a lot of kids. Some were street kids who heard they could find a safe place to live and get a job that might last; others came straight from prison and resolved not to get caught up in the treadmill of returning to prison. My task now was to return to San Diego and get the statistics to prove we served enough youth.

My first step was to appeal the Ben & Jerry's original decision. More papers? You know it! I asked a man I knew in the Department of Labor's Youth Opportunity Program to write a letter on our behalf. We filed more papers, sent more letters, and discovered that just over 25% of our clients were between 15 and 21 years of age, just the profile Ben & Jerry's was looking for. Okay! We did meet their criteria.

I returned to Vermont and waited patiently for another discovery day. I just knew they would say yes. I met with the CEO. I met with the Senior VP. The day was sliding by, and no decision was being made. I had a 6:15 flight, but by 4:45 we still had no word. Sometimes I wonder why God sends tests of patience to me and other impatient individuals. Why couldn't He give these tests to people who could pass them more easily? I know they are out there. I see them at the grocery store, just standing there and looking into space. They are not tapping their fingers, jiggling their keys, or rearranging the magazines. They are just *waiting*. Calmly. Patiently. So, why me? I'm not Job.

At 4:46, (yes, I was counting the minutes as they ticked by) the Senior VP finally looked over the table and asked, "Scott, why should we do this?"

One thing I have etched into in my head, into my cells, maybe into my DNA is always, always, always to know why I want the *Yes*. I knew the answer in every cell of my body.

It took me no time to reply, "We have spent over nine months filling out papers and waiting, answering questions and waiting, collecting and sending data, and waiting, as we were asked to do. We have flown here twice and waited for a very long time. This is hard-won because we really want it. We need this opportunity to help serve our population. With your brand, we can open doors." I left the black and white cows and Ben & Jerry's with a franchise agreement. We ran the store for more than four years.

We came up with some creative, imaginative innovations. One of them was the "Fire Drill Day." I noticed one day that the management companies of the tall buildings downtown would have regular fire drills for their tenants. The problem was that the tenants knew they were drills, and many of them would stay at their desks instead of tromping down long flights of stairs. This did not look good to the Fire Marshall.

This was a great chance for us to apply some creative brain exercise. How could Second Chance and our Ben & Jerry's franchise create a win-win solution for the management companies? The answer was quite simple. The owner bought ice cream cones for everyone who participated in the fire drill. We discounted the price, our very proud Second Chance graduates scooped ice cream, the tenants cooperated, and everyone was happy. It really was fun. And we made money. Everyone came out ahead.

A few years later, we decided to sell the franchise. Fat was in the news, and a local channel "interviewed" a rack of ribs and an ice cream cone. Which had more fat? Which could clog those old arteries more quickly? The rack of ribs won with less fat; the ice cream lost. Now that fat-conscious consumers were better off eating ribs than ice cream, the ice cream business everywhere started to decline. One lesson I learned from my parents was always to know when it's time to get out. We sold the franchise for what we paid for it. And yet, for four years we had a lot of fun and did a lot of good things.

Start by Noticing

Thinking outside the box is not a skill that belongs to only a few chosen individuals. We are all wired to create. Creating is not just writing stories, painting pictures, or inventing the newest software. Creating is coming up with solutions to problems. The Fire Drill Day was not initially outside-the-box thinking. It began with noticing. I noticed groups of people standing outside the tall buildings, and I asked, "Why?" Then I wondered why, for such tall buildings, there were not that many people. I asked a lot of questions. What did people need? Cooperation. What did people want? Incentive. We noticed, then we acted.

So many people give up so easily.

"Oh, well. It didn't work the first time."

"The contact never called back."

"Someone thought it was a stupid idea."

"Mom or dad never did it like this."

These are all just excuses and lies that people tell themselves to stay in their comfort zones. I have learned to keep trying, and to not be afraid to try something different or new. After all, if it took Edison almost 1,000 tries to come up with the light bulb, surely I'm good for more than one. So, instead of making excuses, I might:

- call the contact at a different time of day
- ask someone else to help me figure it out
- tell the name-callers to get lost
- try something bigger

This effort is part of evolution. I look around, and I see that life expands. That is what we are meant to do. Expansion and growth and creativity bring us fulfillment, completion, and happiness! It's all so natural.

Pop!

Our world, big or small, gets squeezed so often by the pressures of challenge, struggle, and fatigue. I can almost hear humanity let out a collective moan, "That's it. Nothing can be done. It's hopeless." It's like the doctor who says, "Well, it's just part of getting older. There's nothing we can do about it." I hear that and I think, "No, there *is* something to be done. We just don't know what yet." But then, on top of the moaning and the sighing and the resignation, something pops.

Suddenly, magically, divinely, someone somewhere sheds a new light on a problem that lets him see a new way of approaching or understanding the same old events. Like a bursting kernel of popcorn, the unconscious pressure has popped a new idea into existence, and the world is no longer flat.

In the past, when I bumped up against a seemingly immovable challenge, my automatic reaction would have been, "I'm screwed!" I rarely have that reaction any more because I have *experienced* breaking through the challenges, moving around the *no's*, and learning that what seems to be a huge stone block in the road is, in actuality, nothing more than the impetus needed to produce the *pop.*

This *pop* has almost become a game for me. I love wrestling with, "How often can I change what hinders me into something that helps me? How can I get to *Yes* when I am being told *no?*" There are times when I tell myself to stop playing games. But, even when I cannot imagine what that something might be, I still like playing the game. Life itself is the biggest game of all, and I truly love to play.

Even fundraising can be a game. Money is always a game. Always. How will I get it, where will I get it, who will give it to me? The non-profit I run is truly a non-profit. There are times that we have to wait for a donor check to clear before we can meet payroll. Yet we always make it. I know we will always make it and the staff knows we will always make it, but there is still drama that makes the whole thing exciting. I must love drama, or I would not be doing what I am doing.

Now that I know there is always a way, my dramas typically have good outcomes. But it was not always like this. Years ago, when I was ruled by my temper, my dramas had painful consequences and regrettable outcomes. But by the grace of God, those days are long gone, and I can't imagine how tedious life would be without some drama.

I've had business leaders, politicians, celebrities, and friends ask why I work in the non-profit field when I have the drive and talent to succeed in any business I choose, big or not so big. They ask "Why don't you do something that makes you a boat load of money?" I *do* make boatloads of money, I just never take it home at the end of the day. I use it to buy safe houses, purchase computers to train my people, and build more classrooms. And on most days, I have a boatload of fun doing this. The drama and the excitement are worth far more than a boatload of money to me.

Fun

For me, it has to be fun, too. A lot of people do not agree. For them, other things are more important, such as the acclaim and prestige, the security brought by money, or the power. I know that at times they shake their heads or see me as less than mature. So what? Another of my mottoes is "Do some good. Have some fun." That may be too simple to some people, but for me, it's perfect.

You must know the classic saying about teaching people to fish instead of *giving* them fish. If I had to *give* fish to thousands of men and women, I would not have the cash, the energy, or the passion to do it. Maybe I could raise the money, but why? It would not juice me. It would not fire my passion and focus. It would not be fun. My *Yes* is to help others help themselves. I dive right in. That's the only way I know. And that makes it fun. Being fully engaged and 100% present is fun.

I do it all because I like to do it and I want to do it, not because I will earn points in heaven, make a lot of money, or please other people. I sure don't do it for the jet-set life, which I do not live. I do it because it is what I am designed to do. I feel like I am flying, and I love it.

My Mom

A few years back, my mother, Maggie Silverman, looked at our local community, saw something lacking, and began to imagine and implement a solution to the problem. She figured out what was needed, and she stepped up and followed through.

She noticed what thousands of other people noticed. The difference was that my mother came up with something no one else considered. She took it upon herself to put the wheels in motion to address the need she and others saw. Out of respect for the victims, she acted.

What she saw was that not every citizen of San Diego lived an abundant life, especially those who were hungry. So my mother decided that our family would make baskets of food and goodies to distribute on Thanksgiving. She set up long tables in our garage to assemble the baskets, gathered some friends, recruited all her family, and we came together to created festive, brightly decorated baskets that held everything a family would need for a tasty holiday meal.

This was not a Temple project or a city-wide women's club project. This was a Maggie Silverman project. She made it happen, then she enlisted local police officers to deliver the completed food baskets. I sometimes wonder what would have happened had she gone into the non-profit arena instead of retail clothing. She *never* thought of *no*, only *Yes*.

That first year, we fed forty families. Four years later, we fed four hundred families. My mother's deep respect for others and her belief that she could change her world drove her to change what she wanted to change. She was clear, and she was focused. Never did she say "the problem is too big even to start." She just started and kept at it, and it grew. That is the power of living from *Yes*. My mother embodies this power.

During the days when civil rights was a frequent topic of preachers, the Temple my mother belonged to occasionally had guest speakers. On one particular Shabbat, the guest spoke of the need for jobs for women of color. He challenged those listening to change what he saw in the community—a vast sea of white faces. Always one to respond to a challenge, Maggie put together a new program at our family's stores to train 20 black women in retail selling. At this time in history, retail selling meant real customer service and complete product knowledge. She personally selected the twenty candidates and gave them a training that lasted four days. On graduation day, friends, family, and a select group of customers were invited to the stores to witness the integration of San Diego fine clothing. Maggie then sent these 20 women out into the community to interview and be hired by other retailers. She held several other classes for women of color and continued to bring integration to the San Diego area. Every time, Maggie beamed as broadly as each of the ambitious, hard-working graduates. This was new to them all. It was new to San Diego. But not to us. We knew this was just what Maggie did.

My mother is not a woman who takes *no* as an end to a goal, but rather as a word that inspires the question, "How do I do this?" She doesn't know barriers as anything more than bypasses on the road to *Yes*. If she calls and invites me to a fundraiser or a community event and I decline, she calls Michelle and asks her to talk to me. While Michelle was talking to me, my mother would call my two sisters and two brother-in-laws and enroll them in what she was arranging. With a mother like Maggie, it is no surprise to me that *Tell Me No. I Dare You!* is my mantra.

Maggie inspires the commitment to doing whatever it takes to get done what your gut tells you must get done. I am amazed at how much organized energy society devotes to encouraging conformity, condoning cover-your-butt decision-making, and stifling the human urge to do what they we are designed to do—create. I sit in long meetings where interminable hours are spent defending old, slow, and ineffective approaches and new ideas are dismissed before they are even tried. I have heard "But we've never done that before!" so many times that it makes me sick. If something is not working, look for a different approach or a better way. There is always a way. Always.

Remember:
- Winners are willing to do whatever it takes (without breaking laws or causing harm) to achieve their vision
- Achieving your goal requires creativity
- There is no frickin' box!
- When someone says *no*, let it launch a new *Yes*
- The pressure of *no* lets ideas pop
- Turn challenges into the "*Tell Me No, I Dare You!*" game
- Make the work you do for your *Yes* fun
- There is always a way. Always!

CHAPTER 11

Second Chance

In the early days of Second Chance, I looked up from my desk to see my 1:30 appointment standing at the door of my office. It was 1:45, and being late does not make for a good first impression. As I attempted to make eye contact with him, he spit out, "They tell me you can help me get work." Hmm, I thought, late, and with an attitude.

"Sit down and let's talk about it."

His response: "I don't want to sit down and talk about it! I just need a job."

I took a breath, reminding myself that in his world, he knew things I didn't know. "You've been in *my* office twenty seconds, and all you've done is offend me and piss me off with your attitude. You have walked across *my* crib, so like I said, let's talk about it. Tell me your work history."

"I don't have one."

"What have you done?"

The angry answer came out with a vengeance, "I've been in jail most of my life."

I slowed my speech down and said, "Do me a favor and back off me; take your attitude and put it in your pocket for a second because I am here to help. *And I want to remind you, you walked into my office.* So, I want you to lower your tone with me. Whatever your problem is, I'm not part of it. If you push me, then I *will* become part of it. So, tell me about your work history."

"I don't want to talk about it. It's nobody's business."

"Why don't you just leave?" I looked him straight in the eye. Even though he was still looking down, I let him know with my look that I respected who he was and I respected myself enough to not waste his time or mine. "You don't want any help, so you might as well leave."

He turned on his heel and marched out of my office. A moment or two ticked by, then his face was back in the doorway.

"Look, I'm so frustrated." he confessed. "People ask me over and over again the same questions. I don't have answers, and nobody wants to help. They just want to ask the same questions."

"Do you think your attitude could have something to do with why people don't want to help?"

He looked at me for the first time. I had him. He sat down.

"So, tell me, what were you in jail for?"

"Robbery."

"Did you use a weapon?"

"No."

"How many times did you re-offend?"

"Six." Now he looked down.

"How many years in jail?" My tone stayed neutral. I could have been this guy, I thought, so no judging allowed.

He told me he had spent seventeen of the last twenty years in jail.

"So, each time you got caught, what was it for?"

"Robbery, but I never once used a weapon."

"Let's talk about this. First, you have *got* to be a great communicator because you have been convincing people to give you their money. Second, you don't use a weapon, so you must be really, *really* good at selling yourself. So, now we know, you've got great communication skills. You're a good salesman. Let's see if we can get you a job in retail."

The tough guy look disappeared; visibly, he began to relax, and then a trace of a smile showed at the corners of his mouth. His dark eyes brightened, as though he had just seen something for the first time. I had entered *his* world. I had shown him respect.

"We found something you do well. Let's see if we can get it transformed into the mainstream."

He eventually got a job with a large manufacturing organization and was promoted to the sales team.

It took about twenty minutes to disarm him.

I could have yelled or told him he was a fool, that he was stupid, and that I was his only hope. Not only would that have separated us, but I didn't believe it. I believed he had useful skills that were simply misplaced, and I saw that he was using familiar behaviors to survive in the world in which he lived. I never said the skills themselves were harmful or that the consequences of those behaviors were wrong. Redirection was all he needed.

I believe that if people commit crimes, they need to be stopped. I also believe that all of us have skills and behaviors that help us survive and that these skills can be modified to help us not just survive, but thrive.

"Let's talk about what you would really love to do as a volunteer," I often say. "And then we can find someone to pay you to do what you would do for free."

That is the process I used with him, and that is the process my team and I always use with our clients. We meet the person where they live, show them how we live, and invite them to join us. We let them know they do not have to join us or live in our world, but we assure them we are not going to live in theirs. We give them a new option. We respect their right to choose, and we trust that if we provide the proper environment and treat them with respect, they will hear their own *Yes* and make a healthy choice. Over the years at Second Chance, we have learned that this approach works almost all the time. Respect is the most efficient catalyst of change.

A Three-week Commitment

If you visit Second Chance on a day of opening orientation, you'll see approximately one hundred guarded, defensive individuals, their eyes darting, with "tough guy" written on their foreheads. The first test we throw at them is being on time. We tell them that we start at 9:00 a.m. and at 9:01 they are late. No excuses. We make sure there is a consequence for being late, a consequence for using profane language, and a consequence for not finishing assignments. No excuses. In the real world of being an employee, excuses do not work. Finishing assignments, being on time, being respectful—these things work. Are they committed to getting a job? Are they willing and committed to changing their future? Are they committed to *Yes?* If so, they are willing do what it takes. If not, they will still be committed to something. We are always committed to something, even if it is apathy. The question is always what that commitment will bring. They tell the trainers they are committed to changing their lives, getting jobs, getting a future. We want to believe them, but we still make them demonstrate it.

If you come back three weeks later, you will see a unified group of men and women who say, "Excuse me," "Thank you," and "Good Morning." When they say these words they look you in the eye and hold their heads high. They may disagree with each other, they may question the trainers, and sometimes they may look at me with a bit of doubt or curiosity. "What's his game?" they may think. But they don't get in each other's face, and they don't attempt to intimidate one another. There's no need to intimidate when you are sure of yourself and your worth and you have a healthy self-respect.

A recent group of graduates included a kid of nineteen covered with tattoos. His burning wish was to be a world-renowned tattoo artist. He'd been in and out of prison and juvenile hall, and he knew all the gang symbols. In the same class, we had a fifty-two-year-old woman who had been using heroin on and off for years. She'd had never been locked up, but the only way she knew to was to manipulate and deceive. Her dream? To work at Second Chance and give back what she received. We also had a veteran of numerous prisons. The forty-eight-year-old's dream was to get a job where he could use his knowledge of math. He learned to smile during the three weeks he was with us. He had not smiled before because he was missing most of his front teeth. During our Handshake 101 class, he smiled at and shook hands with over 100 other smiling individuals. At the end of that day, still smiling, he asked his landlady for an extension on his rent. He got it. In the past, these three very different individuals would have been adversaries and have avoided each other. Here at Second Chance, they came together and realized they had more commonalities than they had differences.

Our participants do not have a lot of time to learn to take responsibility for what they do, what they say, or what their body language communicates. The personal growth industry has grown since I first began Second Chance. Today, there are year-long and two-year long programs to empower individuals to get what they want, change their lives, and take a different path. Second Chance students have three weeks. If they want a job, they had better change their superior attitude, their victim attitude, their chip-on-the-shoulder attitude and do it quickly. If they don't, no one will hire them. As an additional incentive, they also understand that our trainers may ask them to leave if they don't shape up.

Darlene

One of our graduates, Darlene, was incarcerated at Las Colinas Detention Center when she first heard about Second Chance's new Prison Reentry Employment Program (PREP). Our staff had been making visits to Las Colinas to speak with inmates about the new program, and Darlene came to every presentation. The third time she showed up, Lila and I asked her if she would be interested in applying to be the first female PREP participant.

Las Colinas is a detention center for women in the heart of Santee, a town of about 50,000 in the eastern part of San Diego County. The center, originally built for about 300 female inmates, houses close to 700. Expansion is necessary, but Santee residents are not too keen on more felons living on fifteen acres in the middle of their city—a very familiar story.

On the day of Darlene's release, Lila met her at the gates of Las Colinas and took her directly to a classroom at Second Chance. She was in the same wrinkled clothes she had worn when she went to prison. Inmates are given whatever they wore into prison to wear on the outside as they leave, which seems like a great reminder of who they were and an unspoken invitation to return to their old ways. If no one on the outside brings them fresh clothing, they wear what they had on two, three, or ten years ago when they were locked up. I wonder what would happen if they got cleaned up before they left.

When Darlene arrived, she would not meet the eye of our trainer or any of the participants. She would not look at our Wall of Success. Darlene told me a few years ago that she felt superior as she looked around the room. She smiled as she told me this. "Imagine, *I* felt superior! I was just coming from being locked up; I had the look of a crazy person, and *I* felt superior."

Darlene had an attitude bigger than any of the men she was teaming up with. She went around and around, bumping up against one consequence after another. A necessary step in moving out of the victimized, everyone-is-against-me mode is learning that actions have consequences and that the individual can direct his or her thoughts and actions in new directions. Darlene also she learned about body language when her own mother finally told her, "Your mouth is closed, but your body is still talking." Hooray for Darlene's mother!

Darlene is not sure when or how it happened, but she told us that all of a sudden, a light bulb came on and she saw her lie. "I knew what I was doing was wrong, but it had worked for me, so I convinced myself it was right. I told myself I was right, and the laws were wrong, others were wrong, the trainers were wrong, my 'coworkers' were wrong. Once I admitted to myself that what I was doing was just not right, I decided to change or at least to be willing to change and to listen to what might work for me. I got real willing to learn."

When Darlene completed the three-week program, she spoke to the class, her friends, the dignitaries, and her family. "Today I feel good on the inside, and good on the outside. In the past, I would smile out of fear. Today, I smile because I have accomplished what I set out to do. I was chosen to be in this program; I participated in this program, attitude and all; and I completed the program." Her voice softened, and you heard her heart doing the talking. "I look back at my life, and I was never first at *anything*." She looked out at all the people listening to her words. "Now, I am. I am the first female participant and *graduate* of PREP."

That was six years ago, and Darlene is still accomplishing, still smiling from the inside out, and still taking responsibility for what she creates. The wrinkled clothes are gone. At a recent graduation—she often comes to the to cheer people on—she had on a grey suit and heels and looks like who she is—a gifted woman of warmth and character who knows she can help others.

Modeling Respect

Someone recently asked me how I taught respect. The question caught me by surprise. I had never realized I was doing that. I thought I had been getting people ready to interview for a job and to begin to take responsibility for their *lives*. It hadn't occurred to me that I was teaching respect.

Webster gives several meanings for the word, among which are a few that I gravitate toward:

- Esteem for or a sense of the worth or excellence of a person
- To hold in esteem or honor
- To show regard or consideration for: *to respect someone's rights*

It is tough to respect yourself when you respect no one and no one respects you. At Second Chance, we do teach respect. We teach it every day. When I am at a restaurant, I teach respect. When I am at the grocery store, I teach respect. Whenever and wherever there are people, I teach respect. *Tell Me No. I Dare You!* includes the quality, "I respect you and what you stand for." The world is starving for dignity and respect. Give it dignity and respect, and the whole world will say "Yes."

Remember:

- Self-respect is a fast ticket to *Yes,* commitment, willingness, endurance, and faith in oneself
- Self-respect enables respect for others
- Respect disarms and replaces attitude
- Respect is a cornerstone of Second Chance

Respect is so much more powerful than fear. This seems simple and obvious, so why is fear still used as the prime motivator in education and personal growth programs? We explore this question in the next chapter.

CHAPTER 12

Respect

I believe that respect is one of the most important ways *Yes* shows itself, and yet it is also one of the most overlooked necessities of life. Respect is not just what you show to others. It is also what you show yourself. Without self-respect, in fact, you can't fully respect others.

Today, I try to model respect. In my earlier days, I may have been polite and aware of the consideration I was supposed to show others. But I had not yet gained real respect for myself, and that lack manifested itself in my outer world. I instinctively looked at others with distrust. Whenever I entered into business with anyone, my first thought was "How is this person going to try to screw me?" When that thought starts coloring your mind, your radar looks for proof that your suspicion is well-founded. You start hearing in a very selective way. You look for clues, for ambiguous statements that could let you know another person's real intentions. And, just like when you look for success and failure, when you look for demons, you'll find them. It takes a lot of energy to be so vigilant. It's mentally and emotionally exhausting. But, if you insist on keeping your guard up, you have no choice but to spend the energy.

What was even worse for me was that my suspicions turned inward against myself, "What is so wrong with me that I would let someone get close enough to hurt me?" I don't believe I actively decided to shun respect and trust, but my temper colored many of my judgments. It got me what I wanted, usually, but it did a lot of damage to me personally. I smoldered in wariness and defensiveness, ever vigilant and ready to explode. I felt like a jerk when my outburst of temper was all over. But it was the only way I knew to get what I wanted, so I thought I had no choice. The real pity was that I injected so much poison into my relationships with everyone I came in contact with that they didn't want to be around me any more than they had to. I was like a lumberjack who thought he could yell at trees until they fell.

STRIVE

Thanks to Second Chance and my twelve-step meetings, I was able to change my outlook. Thanks, also, to Michelle for alerting me to what seemed like a perfect opportunity. In 1999, Michelle called me to the television to watch a *60 Minutes* feature segment about a program in Harlem known as STRIVE (Support and Training Result in Valuable Employees). It was a job-readiness program. I decided on the spot that I wanted the program for my agency. I set out to get it.

I pursued STRIVE the same way I was learning to pursue all my goals—with an obsession, an unwavering determination, and a whatever-it-takes attitude. The *Yes* I felt while I was watching the program had me vibrating. It was all I could think about as I wrote letters and made phone calls. My obsessive/compulsive tendency was directed and focused, my blinders were on, and my *get- to-Yes* was at full throttle. I persisted. I persevered, I even forced myself to be patient. It took me 90 days just to get through to a decision maker. It took every bit of discipline I could muster not to use my temper to wake up the people who were asleep at the other end of the phone line. So I stayed committed, kept calling, kept nudging, and, most importantly, kept seeing the *Yes* that I knew was possible.

Persistence paid off. One year later I was on my way to Harlem for my own training in STRIVE. Could there could have been a shorter way, a quicker route? Did it have to take so long to get what I wanted? Perhaps. But I was off drugs, time wasn't so urgent, and I was finally on my way.

Today, I weigh about 210. I am 5'11", and I look okay for a fifty-four year old man. When I went to Harlem and began the training in 2000, I weighed 320, and I was still only 5'11". I was a big, white, Jewish wannabe diving into a community of tough blacks who had to find out what I was made of.

Grasping the STRIVE training involves experiencing the training the way a client does. So, during my training, I was the "client" and some guy dressed in a suit was my "provider." I felt like an outsider in every way imaginable. I looked different; I talked different; I acted different; I even thought I heard different, if you can understand that. When people spoke, sometimes I felt as though I was listening to the words of a foreign language. Certainly, I felt like no one knew me. I had the experience of being pre-judged, ordered around, pigeon-holed, and then judged some more. I was not asked what I wanted; I was told what someone else wanted from me. Always, always, always, the words were caustic. I experienced what it must feel like to be a twenty- or thirty-year-old, wise in the ways of living on the street and surviving a lock-up, who is thrust into a world where the language is strange, the customs are bizarre, and people judge them for what they don't know instead of what they do. The lesson hit home: just because I knew how things were in my world did not mean I knew how things were in someone else's.

Part of respect is being willing to admit I do not know another's world while remaining willing to learn what I can about it. This is what Webster may have meant by showing "regard or consideration for: *to respect someone's rights*" My time in training through STRIVE reaffirmed to me that it is impossible to earn someone's trust when you spit at them all weekend. It was great training. I came back to lily-white La Jolla, California with a profound respect for what I did not know. And as I grew in respect for others and for their "worlds," I noticed that I also grew in respect for myself. "What goes around comes around" is true in more ways than one.

"Shut the F--- Up!"

I made a second trip to Harlem some time later for an orientation with a live observation. I was excited to get this transformational program up and running in San Diego, so I made lists of questions, phoned to get answers, and generally nudged and pushed and pestered. Time and time again, I was told to wait until I got there. I waited. Not happily, but I did wait.

When I got to New York and returned to STRIVE headquarters in Harlem, I was still the fat white Jewish guy, but this time, I felt more comfortable in this land of black and fit. I turned into an information sponge. I even stepped out of character for me and took notes during my time there. I was intent on getting it all down in detail.

A group of us were taken by bus to observe a STRIVE training. My enthusiasm had me bouncing from foot to foot in anticipation of getting real answers to the questions I had on my pad of paper that were left over from the last visit. I was closing in! I was pumped!

As we lined up for the bus, I introduced myself to the woman who was counting us and getting us all up and in and seated. I took out my pad and asked her if I could ask a few questions. I told her who I was, that I was from San Diego and was going to be running STRIVE at my Second Chance Agency. I kept up a steady stream of statements about me and questions about

STRIVE. I did not look to see if she was paying attention. The questions just kept flying out of my mouth. When I stopped to take a breath, she stared at me with a look of utter contempt and said the words I had heard way back in 1984 at the treatment center: "Shut the fuck up and get on the bus!"

My first thought was, "These people are not very nice." I did as she said, but did I really need to hear this?

Hadn't she heard my questions? Didn't she grasp the seriousness and the magnitude of their importance? Didn't she know how many lives this was going to make better, how many social problems it was going to solve? Had she no clue what was at stake? I got on the bus wondering if this wasn't some bizarre part of the training. I resolved to just do what I was told and get what I needed to get. What I wanted. But I didn't like it.

I left Harlem drained. The intensity, the screaming, and the unending degradations exhausted me. I knew it was training, and I knew it would help me understand what my clients may have gone through elsewhere. Still, it took all I had to stay connected to who I knew myself to be and to keep my self-respect intact while I continued to respect those who were training us. I spent many hours contemplating the fact that many of our systems scream, yell, punish, shame, and limit the very people they are supposed to serve, and then they wonder why those individuals return to jail, fail tests, stay on welfare, or remain completely unequipped to join society. I believe if there was respect for the uniqueness of each human being in all of our systems, we would have a better world.

No Fear

Face it, fear works. If I scream at a group of people long enough and hard enough and scream at them at every turn, they will become afraid and eventually do what I want them to do. At least for a certain amount of time. Slavery worked, dictatorships work, prodding with an electrical rod works. They all work until someone bigger or meaner comes along. They all work until a larger fear emerges. Scream at someone long enough and they may do what you want, but you can bet that they will avoid you in the future, and there will be no relationship fostered.

The way I see it, we all share the world. Your rights are just as important as mine, and my rights are just as important as yours. I can respect myself and respect you at the same time. That's why our groups at Second Chance are not based on fear at all. They are based on reality, consequence, and respect. We have an unwritten creed that each person has value, and that value will emerge if watered and fed. If I were trying to grow a rose bush, I would not go outside every day and shout, "Make something of yourself! Stop with the thorns, they hurt! Hurry up and produce! What is wrong with you? Why can't you be like Sam's rose bush?!" I could do that, but I'd look like a lunatic and the rose would probably die.

The Homeless Man

Second Chance used to attract the homeless, nameless, disenfranchised, and unwanted of San Diego. At times they would even sleep in front of our building. We are located in an area of town where the people we service can get to us easily. To a New Yorker, this area may look like a nice upscale area of San Diego, but we are close to the neighborhoods where our constituency has been living, and it is not always beautiful.

Several years ago, one homeless, nameless man took up residence outside our building. He would be there most mornings when I got to work. If he were awake, I might share a few words with him and send him on his way. If he were asleep, I would nudge him awake him before the class arrived. One morning I stepped around him. He looked sound asleep, and I was running late for an important meeting. After the meeting,

I went out to my car and the homeless, nameless guy was still there. Still asleep.

"Hey buddy," I said as I tried to wake him, "come on, time to get moving."

No movement. I spoke a little louder and more forcefully. Then I called the paramedics—the homeless, nameless guy was dead. When did he die? Was he dead when I walked past him in a rush to get to my meeting, or did he die outside on the sidewalk while I was inside sitting in a chair? I never knew the answer, and I never knew his name.

That homeless guy was once a little boy. Maybe he, too, built a tree house where he felt safe. Maybe he, too, experienced people who yelled and tried to stomp out his fire. Maybe he, too, lost his self-respect and decided to stomp out the *Yes* fire that once burned bright in him before someone else did. Maybe he just gave up and quit. Maybe he believed the *no* he heard. At any rate, he died alone on a sidewalk,

Something Just Ain't Working

Early on, I learned to survive by tucking who and what I was deep inside and letting a hard veneer of anger and rebellion keep the real me out of sight. When the drugs and drinks came along, it was much easier to keep my spark hidden by forming allegiances with others who related to my anger and liked the fact that I was funny when I got stoned. We all tucked our human selves deep inside and said, "Try and scare me now, I don't care."

During recovery I was able to admit that I do care. I care a lot. I care so much I find the waste of human potential intolerable. One of the saddest and most infuriating realities in today's world is that kids kill themselves every day. It took me almost thirty years to reach the end of my rope, where I thought about suicide, but these kids, who are half of thirty, get up on a Tuesday morning and decide that living one more day is intolerable. They make conscious, pre-meditated decisions to leave sunsets, laughter, dancing, pasta, and hope behind and even to take other fledglings with them.

Could this be a clue that something just ain't working?

Johnny

Johnny's story illustrates what we do without thinking to our kids (and our adults).

Little Johnny loved to draw and color. Every birthday he received reams of fresh white paper, boxes of multi-colored crayons, and shiny paints. Each day he would sit with his paper and crayons and make beautiful pictures for Mommy, Daddy, his dog, and anyone who came to visit. Johnny also loved going to school. His big friend Tommy took the bus every day, and Johnny looked forward to the day when he would get on that bus and be big, too.

That day finally came. Johnny went off on the big bus. He had a new backpack. Inside the backpack was a new box of sixteen crayons, a super-hero pencil box, and a surprise lunch Mommy had packed for him. His name was spelled out in six different colors on his lunch bag. He could hardly sit still but he knew the rule was to sit still, so he sat very still on the bus and then again in his seat inside the big school.

He put his crayons inside his desk and put his super-hero pencil box on top of his desk. His teacher stood at the front of the room and said, "Boys and girls, take out your crayons. I will pass out the pictures of flowers we are going to study and color." Johnny was thrilled. Big school, and he got to color! Johnny started to color right away. "Wait, class until I tell you to start."

Johnny put his crayon down and waited.

"Okay, begin."

Johnny looked at all the different colors that lay in front of him. He picked up a crayon that looked like a beautiful shade of blue and began to fill in the petals of the flower. Then he picked up a bright yellow crayon and drew lines radiating out from the petals. Johnny chose a neon green crayon and filled in the center of the flower. His teacher was walking around the room watching the children color. Johnny was anxious for her to see how beautiful his flower was turning out.

"Oh, no, Johnny! We don't have green flowers. This is a rose, and roses are red. Color the flower red and the petals green. The stem is also green."

Johnny did as he was told and the teacher smiled.

A few years went by and Johnny's family moved. He went to a new school. The first day of school his teacher passed out pictures of flowers and trees.

"Okay, class, I will give you time to color before lunch." Johnny sat patiently waiting. "Johnny, what are you waiting for?" his teacher smiled at him.

"I need to know what color you want, teacher."

His teacher looked a little surprised as she said, "Oh, my goodness, whatever you want. It is your picture. How will I know what you like or how you see things if I tell you what to do?" The teacher smiled again and moved on to another student.

Johnny picked up his crayon. He colored the flower red, the petals green and the stem green. He left the bright yellow and neon green crayons in the box.

This is only a story, but it is an apocryphal one. We send kids to school, tell them we want them to be smart, have them memorize facts, and tell them to spit out what was fed into them. Then we ask them to solve the energy crisis, find a cure for cancer, and "think outside the box." How can we expect an individual to wake up one day and think outside some box when all his life we have trained him to stay inside the box? Is it possible that the kid who refuses to study spelling, doodles on his math book, and won't join the football team might become the guy who finds the way to peace?

I don't have the answer to this question. My hunch is that someone out there does have the answer, but that person is being told *no*.

No, it won't work.

No, it won't get funded.

No, the parents won't like it.

No, flowers are not that color.

No, we'll lose control.

No, no, no.

To that individual I say, "Dare 'em to say *no*. Then say, 'Kindly be quiet.' Or, 'Please get out of my way.' And if they persist, look them straight in the eye, and tell them with all the quiet force you can muster, 'Watch me!'"

Stepford Kids

When I get the chance to speak about education and schooling and the way they begin the shaping small children, I stress how the institutions in our culture teach children to replace fun with conformity, curiosity with structure, creativity with copying, and self-expression with marching in formation.

When our kids are between the ages of two and five, we brainwash them into limiting the fun. "Get serious. Focus, and wipe that smile off your face. Life is tough. You've got to be hard to survive." I heard that from teachers at virtually every school I ever attended, and I attended plenty of schools. Why does it have to be this way?

I have never understood why reading has to be a nightmare. Dr. Seuss creates a sense of fun with made-up words and bizarre pictures that kids and adults want to read, want to look at, want to enjoy, just so they can say words like *oom-pahs* and *boom-*

pabs and play with ideas such as "howling mad and a hoola baloo." (These are not exact quotes, but they are fun to read, and that was the whole idea.) Dr. Seuss, aka Theodore Geisel, got it. Later in his work, he offered life messages that were fun and purposeful. I would love to have met that guy; I just know he was fun. More fun than, "See Dick run." Why do we turn our schools into torture chambers of shame and humiliation?

Teachers and schools may have type-cast me as stupid, but what did they know? I have always loved to learn. Teach me something in a way I can understand, and I get it. I was born curious. I love to expand my knowledge! I have always wanted to know the whys and hows of things. Don't we all start out with a yearning to learn? Isn't curiosity really an inborn quality? Why, then, do we try to crush it?

What do our kids experience in school? What would a fly on the wall hear? Sit in your seats…look this way…draw it the way I do..say it the way I say it…read what I want you to read? Being required to color between the lines and make the sky blue and the grass green can be so demeaning to any kid with an imagination. Why don't they require kids to dye their hair the same color and cut it the same length? If they want Stepford kids, why stop at school uniforms?

There must be a better way to educate.

Schools are not run the way they were in 1964 when I went to school. Thank goodness! The schools my daughters, nieces, and nephews attended seem much more enlightened. Yet there are still individuals who stomp on the spirit of those who act out, act differently, even act annoyingly. The system isn't working nearly well enough yet. Decision makers have a responsibility to recognize individuality, to foster it, and to *not* to squelch the soul and the spirit of those we are paying them to serve. Unfortunately, we still have a long way to go.

I work with many clients who can't handle the "right" way—

felons, gang-bangers, the homeless. The system didn't work for them, either. Look at the prisons. Look at the dropout rates. Look at the people who sleep under bridges, in alleys, and in abandoned buildings. It isn't working.

Physicists and scientists tell us that we are really just energy. How about using the energy, directing the energy, thanking the energy, and not threatening the energy? I watch new parents— many of whom seem to get this idea—direct their kids' energy without stepping on it or (the current vogue) medicating it. I personally believe that my "live out loud, live to the fullest, take up the invitation to play" energy is exactly what we need to get thousands of men and women off the streets, into jobs, and contributing to our world. We need to respect our children and our future enough to give each child an education based on the dynamic energy of *Yes*?

Remember Mr. V?

A few years ago I attended my nephew's high school graduation. I noticed on the participant roster a name from my childhood. It was Mr. A., one of the few good teachers I had encountered growing up. "Mr. A. I'm Scott H. Silverman, do you know who I am?"

He smiled as he responded, "I know you not only from the many articles I read about the good work you are doing, but I know you from XYZ Private School. You were the kid the school was trying to toss out. I was in the room next door when Mr. V. lost control of you and his temper. I was also in on the meetings held after his heart attack. I remember being the only voice of reason at that time. Manslaughter! They were out of their minds." Mr. A. continued, "I told them: think about it. We absolutely cannot kick a kid out of this school or say that a particular kid caused the heart attack of one of our teachers. We would be the laughing stock of the city." Mr. A. shook my hand then shook his head and walked away.

Who knew? I wish I'd known then that there was one sane adult on my side. Long ago I released the fear I had stuffed inside me back then and the shame I felt as a room full of nine–year-old kids laughed when I couldn't point out the Pacific. Today, I think I am lucky that I never fit inside of that box.

A huge part of living in *Yes* is *not* automatically fitting in. More or less, *Yes* is a call to fit in on the outside. Fit in outside the norms, the customs, the business-as-usual, the everyone-is-doing-it-so-it-must-be-okay group. This is not antisocial. It is authentic. It means not saying *no* when you really mean *Yes* or saying *Yes* when what you want to do more than anything is to say *no* loud and clear.

From Carhops to Senators...

Believe me, I know what it is like to be judged. I know what happens to a person's beliefs, self-esteem, self-confidence, and expectations when they are dismissed as worthless, stupid, fat, or ignorant. I have lived with what happens when people in authority have squashed me down in order to plump themselves up. I know what it is like to feel bitter and have my negative feelings reinforced.

To be judged as inferior is one of the most destructive acts of aggression against an individual, more damaging sometimes than a beating. It is one thing to have your body beaten. It is entirely different to have your spirit beaten and broken. I spent over twelve years in school with people in authority who damaged me instead of helping me.

Those memories remain firmly in my awareness. They govern all my interactions with others. I make sure that getting what I want does not mean taking from another. I make an inner agreement with myself that I will always get to *Yes*, and I will do whatever it takes as long as it results in both the other person and me winning. I know now, thanks to recovery and all I have learned since then, that *Yes* beats in each and every heart on this planet. This allows me to acknowledge the excellence that lives in all of us. I am worthy only to the extent that I acknowledge the worth of others. We are all children of God.

Today, I always look for friends. One of the blessings in my life is that I get to interact with some fairly powerful people. Dignitaries, senators, mayors, heads of large corporations— these are the kinds of people I meet in any given week. I also cross paths with people you've never heard of, people who live their entire lives under the radar of attention. I am proud to make them all my friends. I take pride that I know the owner of the top La Jolla restaurant, share friendships with some of the clientele who dine there, and also stay on great terms with the bus staff and the guys parking the car. They all deserve and receive respect. I take to heart the suggestion, "Judge not, lest ye be judged." I have learned there is both power and freedom in this simple principle.

I may not get you what you want and you may not hand me a big donation, but if I make a friend, I am better off than I was yesterday. We all win. No losers. I strive to create a world through simple, authentic connections that serve others. I believe this is the world that best serves all of us. *Yes!*

Remember:
- Fear works to motivate some people, but at a highly negative cost
- Too many of our systems yell at, penalize, and shame the very people they say they serve, and then wonder why those individuals return to jail, fail tests, stay on welfare, or fail to join society
- Fear works only until someone bigger or meaner comes along
- Rigid education packs children into the box, but social needs demand outside-the-box thinking to solve local

and global problems
- What if we had enough respect for children and for the future to educate each child within the energy of his or her *Yes*?
- Judge not; respect all humanity; aim for win-win

Let's see what it's like to graduate from Second Chance.

CHAPTER 13

My Favorite Day: Graduation

I've had a rewarding life so far. I really like the journey I've been on. One of the highest points has always been Graduation Day at Second Chance. For many of the participants, this is the first graduation of any type that they have ever experienced. Their Certificate of Completion is the first piece of paper they have ever received for successfully completing something. It is huge for them, too.

On this day, as I stand at the lectern getting ready to preside over this exhilarating ceremony, I gaze out at a sea of nervous smiles and well-dressed men and women. Gone are the doo-rags, the baggy jeans, the wife-beater T-shirts, and the distinctive colors. The beards have been trimmed, the hair cut or styled, and the makeup applied sparingly. If I didn't know where I was, I could mistake this for any community meeting in the San Diego area. I feel the pride and self-respect ripple through the room. I look out upon eighty-five individuals who found the courage to say *Yes* to their lives, commit to change, and begin the process of interviewing for jobs that will move them ahead, provide them benefits, and get them actually paying taxes. Some will even come back and write donation checks to Second Chance.

The men are in jackets and ties and polished shoes. The women glow in suits, business dresses, or well-tailored slacks.

They are prepared and ready as they sit in the place where fear and excitement meet. It's contagious, and even my palms are sweating.

I give thanks to the trainers and to the eighty-five individuals who remain from the hundred who entered the program. I admit to all those in the audience that this is not an easy regimen, and I acknowledge that some of them will need to go through the program a second or third time before they grasp the importance of doing whatever it takes to change their life and apply our guidelines. I remind them that "Whatever it takes" is a lot. Undeterred, they move as one, sitting straighter and taller and holding their heads higher. A few look over their shoulders to see if the friends and family who have come to share their success heard what I said. Did they hear how I praised them and said how much guts it took to do what they did? Did they hear how much work and commitment and dedication the graduates gave to the program? Did they hear about all the sacrifices that each participant made? Did they hear about the challenges that each graduate overcame, the courage they needed to get to this moment? Some eyes glisten with tears—mine especially.

I look deeper into the audience and see alumni, past graduates who return once a month to support those who are springing from the nest. These alumni have started a support group that meets once a month; they did this independently of Second Chance. They have cleaned out their own crap and found ways to affirm the worth of each individual. They moved from victim to victor, and the reaffirmation they get in the support group constantly refuels their *Yes*.

As I look over the audience of alumni, staff, dignitaries, and friends of these remarkable graduates, I see Darlene. She's here less and less as her outside obligations grow, but Lila and Miguel still ask Darlene to tell her story to the entire class, or her coworkers as we refer to them. It's great to see her.

Rick

Rick is also here today. Local television channels are covering the graduation, and they've already interviewed him. Rick is smart. He went to college, comes from a good family, and could be Mr. Everyman. In other words, he could be you or me. His story makes for very good news. We are happy that Rick and his story have caught the attention of the news. We want the word to go out. We want people to know about us. We want people to see what is possible.

In February 2002, Rick's wife died of cancer. It had been a fight Rick thought they were winning. When she passed away, Rick wanted to join her, but could not bring himself to commit suicide, at least not directly. He started drinking and light drug use because he found that they dulled the pain.

He then tried what so many people do—he tried to deaden the pain by moving. It didn't work. Pain has a nasty habit of holding on and bringing its suitcase right along with its victims. Rick went to Europe and his pain traveled with him. Rick had held down a good job and saved a few bucks, so he took took his drinking and growing drug habit to Europe. Three years of idleness and substance abuse to kill pain dumped him at the end of his money. His health was deteriorating, and by the time he returned to the States, he was desperate.

Rick needed drugs. What was left of his brilliant mind told him to do whatever it took to get those drugs, which were even more expensive in the United States than they were in Europe. He turned to crime to get his criminalized drugs. He discovered that stealing was easier than trying to work again.

Rick may have been a smart executive, but he was a dumb thief. He was soon arrested for his first offense—drugs, no weapons or violence—and Rick got himself released to a residential drug recovery program. The problem was, Rick had no desire to recover. A residential drug recovery program was not what Rick needed to take charge of his out-of-control life.

Rick got arrested again; this time his case ended up in drug court. Drug court tries to divert non-violent, substance-abusing individuals into treatment. The next step is prison. While he was locked up awaiting his day in drug court, Rick heard Jack, our second-in-command at Second Chance, speak.

"It was something to do," he said.

Rick had not done a good job of proving he could stay sober, so this time the court ordered him to get clean or face prison. He decided he disliked the idea of prison more that he liked getting high. He could not get work because of his background, especially his background of theft. Jack got through, and Rick contacted us and started the program.

"To say it was a humbling experience is a huge under-statement," says Rick. He stayed separate from most of his coworkers and did what he was told as he prayed for any job at all that could lead him to his goal of a job where he could just use his brains. By staying away from drugs, Rick showed himself that he still had a brain and that his brain still worked. His brain was returning, and he wanted a place to use it.

During Rick's second week of his Second Chance program, I went into the classroom. I love speaking, especially to the Second Chance participants. I threw out a challenge: who would speak for the group? By now, Rick had the reputation as the smart guy. The group voted for him to speak. I asked him why I should keep anyone in the program; I saw a lot of laziness in the classroom. What did he have to say about it?

Rick had plenty of experience in boardrooms and sales meetings. He started in with some platitudes about equality and self-worth and a load of other crap that came straight out of his jiving and conniving head. I looked at him and said, "Whatever you are speaking is not from your heart, so it is not worth hearing. *Sit down.*" Rick stood for a couple of beats, and I could see his mask slip off. I could see his pain, but I could also see his determination. He remained standing and, with a quiet power, looked me back in the eye and said, "We all want to be here. Every single one of us." His guard came down, and in that moment, he began not just finding a job, but finding a life.

Eventually, he found a job as a general laborer at $10 an hour. His boss was a former graduate of our program. That's how all of this works—we empower one and that one empowers ten and that ten empowers one hundred, all paying it forward.

Rick worked seventy hours a week. He worked hard. One time, a problem came up over the Christmas holidays, Rick solved it. His company had to keep strict time logs as part of their government contracts. A problem cropped up with the time cards, and the office staff had all gone home. Rick fixed it quickly and even had fun doing it, more fun than he'd had in quite a long time.

Shortly after that the owner called him into his office. "I thought they had decided my past was too threatening and they were going to fire me. The thing I could not figure out is why they would have the owner fire me." Rick sat across the desk from Mr. S., who asked him where he had been and why he was working for $10 an hour when it was obvious he could use his mind. By now, Rick had learned to be honest and to speak from his heart. He shared his story, knowing he could lose his job.

"Look," Mr. S. said, "I don't care what you did yesterday. I care about what you are doing today and what you are going to do tomorrow." The man offered him a different position in the company. Rick took the chance, and two weeks into the new job, got a thirty percent increase in pay, which was already much more than $10 an hour. At the time of his television interview, he had been promoted a few more times. As I write this, Rick is the vice president of manufacturing. He is approaching his old salary, but with new eyes. When he tells our newbies that every day is better than the day before, he means it. When he says he now is about giving back, he means it. It is all from his heart.

85 Yesses

I turn my attention back to the graduation ceremony. It's time to hand out this month's certificates, and I start calling out the names. Each of the eighty-five individuals takes the mike, looks at the audience, and speaks a few words. Our resident tough guy with a history of re-arrests shakes my hand, looks at the group before him, and with genuine emotion slowly chokes out the words, "These are people that care about people. I needed to be cared about."

I cry, the audience cries, my staff cries.

We know how true those words are for every individual in this room. We are living in a world where we all need to be cared about. Mr. Tough thanks all of us again, and then he hugs me. He thinks I did him a favor. He may never know, until he starts giving it back, how much of a favor he has done for me.

Benny

Benny is a great man who works here at Second Chance. He is among those there, dabbing at his eyes. He has elevated himself to where he runs the safe housing for Second Chance. Safe housing assures our participants and others in our community a clean and sober living environment. He has a long list of responsibilities, and he has earned every one of them. He finds houses for us to buy, then he obtains the furnishings for them. He fills these houses with clean and sober tenants, and he trains every house manager. On top of that, he does the books and keeps his records in an organized and orderly way.

In Second Chance, we run a group of safe houses where men and women are able to live up to two months safe and free of charge. These are safe places for them because there are no drugs or alcohol. There is a house manager who leads weekly groups. Every participant in every group is expected to be looking for work, taking classes, and going to meetings. The house manager is a position of substantial responsibility.

Benny was once a gang member—actually a gang leader. He spent his early years in and out of prison. He had a destructive, troubled history. He had overdosed seven times, been stabbed, done time, and at thirty-seven years of age, had no dignity or self-esteem. He owed $38,000 in back child support, and the IRS was interested in him. He woke up one day and wanted something different for his life and the lives of his sons. That day, he found a *Yes*.

I met him eleven and a half years ago. He went through our three-week program at Second Chance while he lived in one of our safe houses. Then got a job in construction. He continued to live in the safe house and soon began to pay rent. Benny started the slow process of paying off his $38,000 debt. He just kept allowing the *Yes* of his life to lead him. His *Yes* was to be a role model for his sons, who were beginning to follow in his old footsteps. He could see where they were headed. He knew the pain of their journey, and that knowledge provided powerful motivation for Benny.

Eventually, his house manager noticed Benny and asked him to help with the running of the house. He showed promise as he was given more and more responsibility, and Second Chance eventually hired him to be a house manager. He gained responsibility as he gained our trust, and he is now responsible for all eight of our safe houses. He has trained and mentored all of our current house managers.

Benny has earned back the respect of his family. He has reached the *Yes* that first woke him; he has self-respect and inner trust and is not only a great role model for his sons and daughter, but also for the thousands of those served by Second Chance.

Staying in a place of *Yes* is no guarantee of safety or happy endings. The truth is, life can suck. Life can take an iron chain and beat the hell out of us. Not long ago, Benny's youngest son was fatally shot in the head. Remember, his kids are a big part of his *Yes*. Nothing could have been more devastating. It would have been easy for him to let go of *Yes*, find the gang members responsible for his son's death and return to *no*.

But Benny's *Yes* is rooted in his deep connection with a church and a Lord. Benny now honors the life of his son by teaching gang prevention through his church. He designed a program called GAME that keeps kids out of gangs. In addition, he began going to prisons with his message and became part of Sober Living in San Diego, a group made up of individuals who manage clean and sober housing. His son's life was taken, but not the memory. That short life will live on as Benny uses his grief to help others, as Benny uses his devastation to fuel his daily *Yes*.

Benny is a man who not only lives *Yes*, but shares and expands it into the world. His story is only one of the thousands that demonstrate the unstoppable force of a *Yes*-driven life. It's as if people receive state-of-the-art power tools to build new relationships, new careers, and better health as soon as they finally acknowledge they are worthwhile and have purpose. All because of *listening to and believing in a three-letter word.*

Every month, every graduation, I witness miracles. I witness the courage in the soul of every participant. I witness the breakthroughs that can only be called divine. I witness what happens when people stand up, speak from their heart, and say, as I say, "*Tell Me No. I Dare You!*" and they mean it.

My hope is that the people I work with do not suffer from the excruciating pain, hopelessness, and suffering that accompany *no*. If they can find a powerful *Yes* early enough and understand the value of choosing to be responsible, they may be able to stay out of prison and stay employed, develop self-respect, and contribute to their community. Many of them do just that. They make huge changes and take the big, dramatic steps that not only turn their lives around, but impact the lives of so many others.

That is why I am so hopeful. Yes, I see half-empty glasses, but I see them as glasses that need only to be filled. I see the people, I know the people, who can fill them. People who have found their *Yes*. If grassroots groups in the communities could find a compelling enough *Yes* for homelessness, domestic abuse, corporate breakdown, and war, then the world leaders would climb on board, and one day, the whole world would follow suit.

The power of finding potential and hope cannot be underestimated. Finding and following a *positive vision* can dynamically change the future for us and our children. At Second Chance and elsewhere, the force generated when one individual stands up, says *"Yes, it is possible!"* and follows that up with action that becomes *Yes* is astonishingly powerful. I know it works.

Solutions will be found when individuals, neighborhoods, and communities come together and identify their common *Yes,* moving them forward together as a unit and cooperating to accomplish their goals. Large groups of people can help their struggling and troubled members by sharing their resources and pooling their time and talent and giving hope and direction to those who need it. Nations can use a global *Yes* to solve the tragic problems faced by impoverished countries. Amazing things can be accomplished when *Yes* is embraced by individuals, groups, communities, nations, and the planet.

If I found *Yes* after all I had been through, there is hope for absolutely anyone. Once individuals have become familiar with living a yes-driven life, they, too, can appreciate the power that goes along with their new discovery. And then they can help others. In fact, I feel strongly that *Yes* creates a desire and a duty to help others. Some people may lead by example. Some may teach formally. And others may work with individuals one-on-one. Whatever people do, it emerges naturally and organically from the choice to live in *Yes*.

There are ripple-effects, too. The ramifications reach out into all sorts of situations, both personal and global. Consider all the tremendous possibilities! I am passionate about fulfilling my responsibility, doing my part, and getting the message out there. I want to make it possible for people to change their lives. I want them to know that their past does not have to hold them back or keep them down. I want more than anything to share the message that there is possibility, there is hope, there is life.

Remember: Everything in life comes down to choices, and we each have the choice to empower *no* or to embrace *Yes*. *No* is destructive. It is stifling. It causes stagnation. *Yes* has the power to change the individual, the country, and the world for the better. The choice should be easy.

CHAPTER 14

Flippin' Tidal Waves

I am sitting here in La Jolla while Michelle sleeps in the next room. The man I am today seems light years away from that nine-year-old who threw avocadoes at the neighbors from the safety of his tree house or the twenty-two-year-old kid in Europe, or the thirty-year-old drug addict poised on a window ledge who thought he knew what life was about. Who I am today even seems far away from who I was when I was scraping together money to get offices and rooms for a few homeless guys.

Never, ever, did I have a clue that one day I would walk by a thirty-nine and a half foot wall of photos of beautiful human beings whom I helped empower. It is Second Chance's Academy Award Wall, an Academy of Courage, lined with the beautiful faces of human beings who found inner courage and now help others find the rewards of their inner courage. Respect graces my life. Visit Second Chance; you'll feel what I feel when I see Miguel leading a group or Benny finding furniture for one of our homes. You'll see people who look each other in the eye and smile at each other when they pass in the hallway.

During the last twenty-four years, my commitments have expanded. My original commitment to sobriety continues to be a priority, and every Saturday morning I am up and out the door by 6:30 a.m. and on my way to a twelve-step meeting. If I need to, I will go to more than one meeting a week, but I am committed to Saturday mornings. Once a week has taken the place of once a day, though I still work on sobriety every day. My new commitments include integrity, health, and balance. I am still giving back and helping others, and the commitments I made twenty-four years ago at the end of two kite strings still define what I now do for a living.

My commitment to family has also shifted and grown. Michelle's support has been steadfast, and she has lived the words she spoke twenty-six years ago: "in sickness and in health." I still marvel that while I was flying kites and volunteering and looking for a future that would support us, she was working and bringing home paychecks. In 2000, I asked Michelle to renew our vows. It was something I knew I owed her, but more than that, after 16 years of sobriety, I wanted to stand with a Rabbi in front of my family and recommit to sharing my life with the woman who is, herself, the personification of commitment. Our original wedding was almost thirty years ago, and I still feel the same about her today.

My family today includes my wife, my daughters, my nephews and nieces, my sisters and brothers-in-law, my parents, and the memory of my brother Gregg. I am committed that his memory will live on through the stories I tell and the love I can share. My commitment to family is my biggest joy. My daughters, Gracie and Jessica, amaze me. They get all this without the need to self-destruct first.

When my daughters were little, I could never take them to school; that was a job for Michelle. I felt like I was delivering my sweet-faced, innocent little girls to the enemy. My eyes would moisten, my chest would tighten, and all my muscles would fill with adrenaline as my body prepared me to rescue the girls from their captors and deliver them from evil. If it had been up to me, I would have gone to school with them every day and stood guard. My job was keep 'em safe and protect their right to decide for themselves what color to paint the flowers.

Jessica just graduated from college. I never went to college, much less got a degree. I was "too dumb," remember? Michelle graduated from UCLA.

Jessica's success flowed out of her own brilliance. There are no words to describe the feeling I had as her name was read. "Jessica Silverman." I had never known a feeling like it. Our Jessica was receiving not one, but two degrees: one for her, one for me. As she walked towards the podium, I saw her taking her very first baby steps, I saw the first day she left me to go to school, I saw her in a beautiful dress for her first dance, and then I saw the day four years before when we brought her to campus for the first time. And there she was, radiant. A young woman. To this day, we disagree about who was beaming more—Jessica or me? Out of many moments in my life, that moment, when they called out her name, could have been the most miraculous moment of all.

And now it is Gracie's turn. She is off to college, where I know she will shine her own light in her own way. And I look forward to seeing the direction she chooses to take, to sharing her accomplishments along the way. I have, in keeping my commitments earned the right to enjoy the success of my children. My commitments have brought me certainty in the power of *Yes*. My commitments have brought me twenty-four years of sobriety. My commitments have brought me Friday nights filled with the laughter of children and old people gathered around the Shabbat candles. My commitments have brought me a special hero honor on CNN with an email from Gracie to everyone she knew: "Check out the CNN Website. My dad is a hero."

Be Willing

Again and again I have been presented with opportunities to grow, to change, to be more than I was yesterday. At each juncture I had to be willing to let go of who I planned to be in order to become the person I was growing into. Always my willingness was being challenged. Was I willing to take the next step? Did I have the courage to do something about which I was uncertain? I am a little wiser now, a little more directed. I still love the edge, yet I strive more for balance as I grow. My edge can now be news interviews on TV and radio. My discomfort is now my nervous tension when I am being filmed or facing a live microphone. I have always been willing to try something new, something different, when times were tough. I still am.

People call me a hero. I'm a hero according to CNN. It is not a comfortable title for me to wear, and it is even tougher to live up to the expectations. I am not sure which is harder: living up to what people expect of me or what I expect of myself.

I continue to be willing. I am willing to be a role model. I am willing to go beyond the normal expectations of a fifty-four-year-old Jewish man. I am willing to go the next place the Universe has waiting for me. I don't expect the challenges or the temptations to stop. I'm in a new and positive comfort zone. Times are no longer tough. Do I want to stop expanding? Not a chance! I have done more for more people than I ever dreamed possible. But is it time for me to rest? No way! Now, am I willing to be out in front of millions and allow my vision to expand? Bring it on!

My willingness will never leave *Yes* or return to *no*. I am determined to keep *"Tell Me No. I Dare You!"* as my mantra. The instant my willingness to change, grow, and be uncomfortable begins to fade, I look around for something else that needs to change. I realize that not everyone is like me. Not everyone is as compulsively driven as I am. I am sure there are people who wish I was not so driven and that I'd relax, take it easy, get comfortable, and stop obsessing. To them I say, "I'm sorry."

But to tell the truth, I am not sorry at all. Too much comfort leads to complacency. It's easy to get complacent with dead-end relationships or dead-end jobs. It's easy to get comfortable and complacent with an out-of-shape body or the homeless we see sleeping in doorways. I know this is true, because a part of me is still tempted to get comfortable, to disappear somewhere, and say "no" when I am asked to do more, give more, be more.

I know that I cannot ignore my *Yes.* The promise of comfort is a false promise. Ignoring my heart is never comfortable. It's a lie. If I believe that lie, before I know it, I will not only be uncomfortable, I will be in pain. It has taken a very long time, but I have finally learned to just be frigging willing! It's easier in the long run.

I have written about my life from a place of *no* and a place of *Yes.* I have not focused on myself to brag. I feel good enough about myself that I don't feel driven to do so. I have written so much about me in order to share the most intimate parts of the process, the parts I know the best. But I have also included stories of some of the people who have embraced the keys to *Yes.* The people I write about could be you, because if *one* person is able to change, *anyone* is able to change. If *one* person is able to find inner greatness, *anyone* is able to find greatness. The best way to access your own inner hero is to say *Yes* to the Universe, commit to a higher vision, listen to the *Yes* that is deep within, and be willing to persevere through discomfort and sometimes pain. Courage and a more daring spirit help, but they are secondary. I did it. So many others have done it. You and people close to you can do it, too.

Be a Hero

Recently, I attended a dinner with more than a few dignitaries and wealthy people. I struck up a conversation with the mayor of a kibbutz in Israel and told him a few of my stories about my adventure in his country. He seemed rather amused at my slant on things, as if he hadn't heard stories like mine very often. But he listened and smiled, and didn't seem too astounded by what I described. Maybe it happens more than I thought.

My daughter Gracie was there and apparently told a few of the individuals about the CNN Hero of the Week piece. While we ate all this fancy food with all the fancy people, the mayor of the kibbutz spoke up, "Your daughter tells us you are a hero. What's that like, to be a hero?" Understand that a mayor in Israel is much like a governor in the United States and more. He is responsible for continuous defense training and preparation for war. This man, who I am certain knows combat and trains people to get underground within fifteen seconds of a threatened attack, asked me what it was like to be a hero.

That was fun, even though I had no idea of how to answer. I knew what it was like to live on a kibbutz, shovel chicken poop, and throw live chickens into a crate. But, what's it like to be called a hero? It is like being called a drug addict (though I'd rather be called a hero). Really, it is only what someone else in the outside world called me. I just do what I see needs to be done, I make sure I am having a good time, so why should I be concerned about how other people label me? Sure, it's gratifying to be called a hero. My daughters are proud of me. My parents and Michelle are proud of me. But the label changes nothing, except I get more emails. So, that's what it's like.

One life. That is all we are given. Even if you believe in

reincarnation, you still have only this one shot to get it right in this lifetime. Every minute of every day is a gift. Ask anyone who has faced death and they will tell you: life is for today. Life is lived not a year at a time but a moment at a time. Who will care when you die that you went along with someone else's idea of how you were to live the life you were given? Maybe you would like a tombstone that reads, "Here lies Harry; he did what we told him and did not make waves." If that is what you want, then grab it, run with it, and be the best non-wave maker you can be. When you are ready to say goodbye to all who are on this planet, you will feel complete. As for me, I want the marker to say, "He made flippen' tidal waves! And we are richer because of it."

Another Thing or Two

Life is a choice. That may seem trite, even simplistic. But, it's also profound and true. The bumper stickers say, "S-- happens." What they don't say is that "S-- happens to every single man, woman, and child on the face of the planet. Pain is not unique. Roadblocks are normal. Disappointments and struggles get handed to all. Some people seem to get way more than others. But no one gets away without any."

The pain that we get is from the *no* we experience. As little kids, as adolescents, as young adults, as middle-aged souls sick of the pain, and as aging citizens of the world who have seen it all, we must choose. When you feel the pain, what do you choose? Do you rebel and scream and lash out at others? Do you retreat quietly inside, thinking you will find safety? Do you look for diversions, distractions, and addictions to dull the pain?

The *choice* you make is completely and entirely up to you. Only you. You can hear *no*, lie down, and give up. You can hear *no* and go out and drink your way to a blackout. You can hear *no* and punch the person who said it. These are some of the choices you can make. No one can take your right to choose away from you. What happens as a result of your choice is simply a natural consequence of what you put in motion when you made that choice.

Do you withdraw and retreat into your cave? Or do you respond with an, "Oh yeah? Watch me!" Do you take the pain and use it to fuel you? Do you turn it into something you can run with, a reason to turn the world upside down? Everyone feels pain at some time. How do you respond? This is your choice.

Does that make sense? If it doesn't, read these words until they make sense to you, then give me a call so we can discuss it.

I had a choice when all around me I heard nothing but *no. No, you can't read...No, you can't amount to much...No, your life is not worthwhile.* At first I chose alcohol and drugs to numb out and not hear the words. I even gave serious thought to getting rid of the *no* by ending my life. When you are dead you can't hear, right?

My choices back then were wrong. I knew it at the time because I felt miserable. Feeling miserable is a good clue about your choice-making. Good choices make you feel good—not high, good. Not-so-good choices make you feel lousy, even when you think you are having one hell of a good time or a great marijuana laugh.

I have been given my second chance. Maybe I've even created my second chance. I don't spend one minute anymore wondering about it. I am way too busy for that. I don't spend the one minute because I have too much to get done.

Some people buckle under and believe the *no* they hear every day of their life. Even they can choose *Yes.* They can find support people or groups. They can join twelve- step programs. They can read and re-read this book. They can give me a call or send me an email.

We all choose. Every day we choose. Even if you don't make a conscious decision, you still choose. My prayer is that no matter what your particular situation, no matter how bleak things may seem, no matter how trapped, beaten, or scared you are feeling, you will find the strength and courage to rise up, face the *no* that surrounds you, take a deep breath, and shout at the top of your lungs, *"Tell Me No. I Dare You!"*

REMEMBER THE 5 KEYS;

- **Know your *yes*.** Spend time with people who believe in you. Spend time in prayer and quiet reflection. Spend time feeling what is right for you. Define it. Understand it. Embrace it. Tell others who you trust what your *Yes* is and write it down. Believe you have a *Yes*.
- **Commitment.** Remind yourself that what you are after is worth getting. Vow that you will do what it takes to get it. "Give up" is no longer in your vocabulary.
- **Be comfortable feeling uncomfortable.** What may seem like a nice, safe, comfortable seven or eight today could prevent you from living at a ten in the future. Let your safety net come from your heart and be aligned with your *Yes*. Getting past *no* is more than worth the discomfort if you can breathe easily and are true to yourself, the most important person you will ever meet.
- **Take the time.** Invest the time. Anything worth doing is worth doing well and worth investing the time. As I say to the people I work with, "Take the time or do the time."
- **Believe that there is always a way.** Ideas are limitless. Believe this. Always believe this.

I invite all of you to play *"Tell Me No. I Dare You!"* Right here. Right now. Use the following form (or make your own) to list all your *no's* and *Yesses*. Email me your results, and then let's talk.

Who/what is telling you *no*?

_____

_____

_____

_____

_____

_____

_____

_____

_____

_____

_____

_____

_____

_____

_____

How can you get to *Yes?*

_____

_____

_____

_____

_____

_____

_____

_____

_____

_____

_____

_____

_____

_____

_____

_____

_____

Scott H. Silverman is available for speaking engagements and holds classes on a regular basis. To reach him, please email scott@scotthsilverman.com.

For those interested in Mr. Silverman's agency, Second Chance, please go to www.secondchanceprogram.org.

SCOTT'S FINAL WORDS

A CALL TO ACTION

Dear Friend,

The journey of my life has been one of ups and downs, crooked paths and beautiful walk ways. There have been the bumps, successes, failures, and endless opportunities.

Writing this book has taken me down a path I had been afraid to travel until my time was right. If you have taken the time to read this book and your life is not where you would like it to be today, take action. If you are afraid to take the step that will lead you out of the no and into the *Yes* waiting for you, write yourself a note. Do it now!

Please visit me at my website, www. Scotthsilverman.com and we will do it together.

No excuses. No barriers. Let's get started!

Love,
Scott